Meg Hutchinson has always loved telling stories, but it wasn't until 1996 that her first novel, *Abel's Daughter*, was published to instant success. Since then she has written twenty-one bestselling novels, and touched the hearts of thousands of fans.

Praise for Meg Hutchinson:

'Hutchinson knows how to spin a good yarn.'
Birmingham Evening Mail

'The mistress of simmering sagas.'
Peterborough Evening Telegraph

'Meg Hutchinson's storytelling skills are attracting a bigger and bigger audience.'
Newcastle Evening Chronicle

MEG HUTCHINSON

A Penny Dip

My Black Country Girlhood

HODDER

Copyright © 2005 by Meg Hutchinson

First published in Great Britain in 2005 by Hodder and Stoughton
A division of Hodder Headline
First published in paperback in 2006 by Hodder and Stoughton
A Hodder Paperback

The right of Meg Hutchinson to be identified as the Author
of the Work has been asserted by her in accordance
with the Copyright, Designs and Patents Act 1988.

1

A CIP catalogue record for this title
is available from the British Library

ISBN 0 340 83758 6

Typeset in Plantin by Hewer Text UK Ltd, Edinburgh
Printed and bound by Mackays of Chatham, Chatham, Kent

Hodder Headline's policy is to use papers that are natural, renewable
and recyclable products and made from wood grown in sustainable
forests. The logging and manufacturing processes are expected to
conform to the environmental regulations of the country of origin.

Hodder and Stoughton Ltd
A division of Hodder Headline
338 Euston Road
London NW1 3BH

My grateful thanks to Tony Highfield for help always so readily given.

Thanks also to Ian Bott and Robin Pearson for consenting to reproduction of photographs taken from their books.

In the Wednesbury of my grandmother's day a 'penny dip' consisted of a slice of stale bread dipped in gravy made with the juices of cooked meats and purchased from the cookshop situated in Union Street.

During the Second World War a 'penny dip' could be got at Purchases' General Store in Dangerfield Lane. This gave two boiled sweets or caramels. How strange, then, that no matter how many times you produced sweet coupons and asked for the monthly ration of one quarter pound of sweets there were never any to be had!

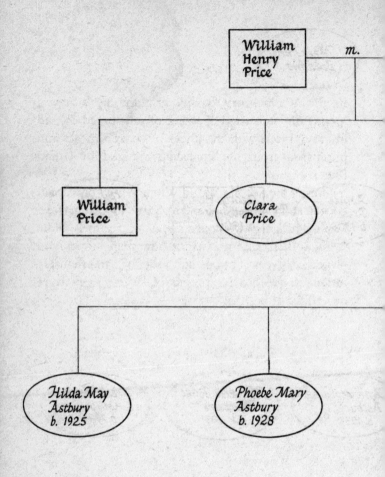

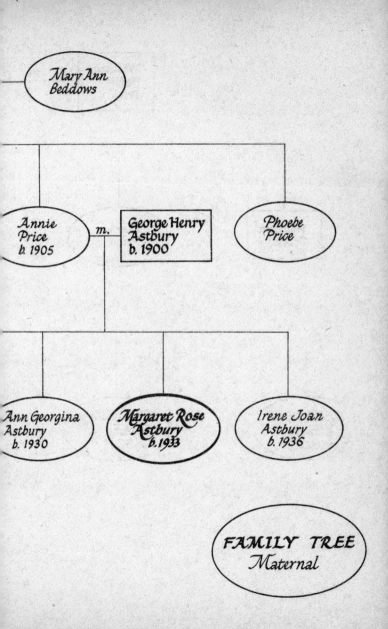

CONTENTS

Contents

I

Portway Road

Although I have written stories of Black Country life at the turn of the twentieth century, colouring them with characters drawn from my imagination, those you will read about in this particular saga were – and are – most assuredly real.

Perhaps I should begin with my grandparents. Walter Edward and Mary Eliza Astbury – my paternal great-grandparents, in fact – had eight children, one of whom, Florence, was the grandmother I never saw and who, as it proved, never harboured a wish to see me or any of the family subsequently born to the son she abandoned at the age of three months.

My maternal grandparents, William Henry and Mary Ann Price, had four children, the third being Annie, born with a paralysed right arm and twisted left leg.

George Henry, the son of Florence, and Annie, the daughter of William Henry and Mary Ann, married and in their turn produced five daughters: Hilda

May, Phoebe Mary, Ann Georgina, Margaret Rose (myself) and lastly Irene Joan.

October 14 1900 saw the birth of an illegitimate baby boy. Born to Florence Astbury, then only seventeen years old, he was taken to live in a tiny run-down terraced house.

Number twenty-six Portway Road was the home and one of a long line of smoke-blackened houses of Florence, her parents and seven brothers and sisters.

What life was like in such cramped, damp conditions cannot be described, but whatever it was, it was not for Florence. Three months after giving birth she abandoned the child.

It might have been an orphanage for George Henry, with no father to claim or support him; that was the usual procedure in the case of abandoned children. But not for George. Florence's parents kept the infant, raising him as one of their own.

The child never saw his mother again.

An unhappy beginning? Of course. Such an introduction to life is not the best for any child but from stories of escapades related many years later it was obvious George Henry grew up well adjusted and happy enough. Nevertheless, when speaking to his own children of Florence, the mother he eventually learned had come to own a boarding house in Blackpool, the woman who never once attempted to contact him, George's eyes could never quite hide the sadness inside.

Holyhead Road Boys' School provided George's education until he reached fourteen. This proved an establishment which brooked no 'cheek'. A leather strap issued swift retribution to any lad daring to answer back when reprimanded or told to do something he didn't want to do, misdemeanours of this or any other sort brought six of the best and worn-through trousers offered little protection to the bottom.

Exceptions were not countenanced at Holyhead Road Boys' School. No matter how poor the family, every boy must arrive each morning in a fresh white paper collar. These could be obtained from John Craven's general store in nearby King Street. But paper collars cost a halfpenny each and from almost his first day at school George had to earn the necessary coin to buy them even though this involved him running errands until nine or ten o'clock at night.

Footwear too was closely inspected and though George's boots regularly had no soles other than those cut from cardboard boxes donated by the same John Craven, the uppers had to be polished until the master 'could see his face in them'.

This headmaster, nicknamed 'Old Nick' by George and the other pupils, would stand at the narrow gateway of the school entrance each morning. There he would consult his pocket watch and at exactly two minutes before nine o'clock would proceed to ring the brass bell held in his other hand. Woe betide any boy arriving after the last peal.

Shuffling along in boots often belonging to his father, George often fell victim to the strap for missing the bell. Laughing over this in later life he would declare 'it were due to me shoes, they was so big I couldn't get 'em past Old Nick stood at the gate'.

Late arrival at school was not always the only reason for boots so big he could hardly keep them on, there was also the business of the penny.

Every evening after supper Walter sent George to buy half an ounce of shag tobacco, the reward being a penny. Every evening this was duly placed beneath the pillow of the bed he shared with Alfred, Walter and Eliza's youngest son. Yet next morning the penny had always mysteriously disappeared. Tooth fairies getting their wires crossed? Not a bit of it. With the boys soundly asleep the wily Walter would remove the coin from beneath the pillow to be produced the next time tobacco was called for.

Continued additions to the family of Walter and Mary Eliza made an already overcrowded house even more untenable and they moved to Ethelfleda Terrace, a cluster of houses grouped close to the parish church of Saint Bartholomew.

Occupying the site of an Iron Age fort raised by

Ethelfleda, daughter of Alfred the Great, then later becoming the place of a heathen temple dedicated to the god Woden, the church stands on a hill overlooking Wednesbury (Woden'sburgh).

This larger house boasted large barrel-shaped cellars, a great place for two boys to play in wet weather. They found it spooky and often would scare themselves with tales of ghosts and ghouls lurking in the shadows. But it was the two very large and very heavy wooden doors closing off the further end that drew them most. Banded across with iron, the keyhole large enough to peep through and see the blackness on the other side, these doors intrigued the pair. What lay through them on the other side? Young minds probed the possibilities, eager eyes and hands searched for the key to those doors which would reveal what magic and the mystery?

But no key was to be found!

Tantalised by boyish dreams of treasure, George decided to ask where it was kept. Putting the question to Mary Eliza, both he and Alfred were taken aback by the vehemence of her answer. They were never, *never* to try opening those doors; in fact they were banned from going into the cellars again.

But Mary Eliza had not realised, or perhaps had overlooked, the fact that bans and boys don't go together. In the case of Alfred and George they certainly did not.

Reluctant to give up their playground, that place of fantasy and promised riches, they continued in their illicit visits. Until caught by Walter!

Chased by Alfred, a lighted candle held beneath his chin while he groaned and moaned, George's half-laughing half-screaming shouts brought Walter to the head of the cellar steps. The boys extinguished the candle with a gasp and froze.

'Be no good served by standin'!' Walter's voice echoed in the silent darkness. 'There be only one way out, you takes it or else you stops where you be – for the night.'

Ghosts and ghouls had been fun when the door to the cellars was open to flying feet, but to be locked in! To climb back up those steps could well end in a hiding . . . But not to climb them! The choice left them no choice at all.

Back in the kitchen, they faced an irate Walter. Hadn't they been told not to go into the cellars?

What was all the mystery?

Bottoms sore from the price of their disobedience, Alfred and George asked themselves the question long after being sent to bed. It was Mary Eliza who whispered the answer. Behind those heavy doors sealing off the cellars was a tunnel, but the tunnel was flooded and in danger of collapse, therefore it must never be entered.

Was there truly a tunnel?

'Oh yes.' Mother would answer her own kids when retelling Father's story. 'It leads straight from Dudley Castle to Church Hill, it was so folk could escape in times of danger; it were along that tunnel the King's men escaped them of the Parliament.'

Cavaliers and Roundheads! What pictures that drew in my young mind, what tales could be told.

Mother enjoyed nothing so much as telling a tale and this was just one more. But this tale persisted, told and retold through the years. As so many times in childhood I would listen but smile to myself and think, 'Come on, Mom, who do you think you are kidding?'

It was not until the seventies Mother's tale was vindicated. Excavations for a new building development in West Bromwich revealed a tunnel fairly deep underground. Archaeological investigation showed it did indeed connect Dudley Hill to Wednesbury Church Hill; it also revealed a network of similar tunnels branching in several directions.

Cavaliers and Roundheads?

Certainly Cromwell ordered Dudley Castle blown up, and yes, various artefacts were excavated, some of which dated from that period. Perhaps Mother's elaboration of a tale had not been such an elaboration after all.

2

Life in Pitt's Square

My mother Annie was the third child of William Henry and Mary Ann Price. Life was hard for many people at the turn of the twentieth century but maybe we can be forgiven for saying that for folk in the Black Country, living their lives in the misery of nail making, sweating fourteen hours a day in steel and iron factories or underground in coal mines, life was just that much harder. How easy, then, for William Henry and Mary Ann to have said raising a child who might never be able to work, to contribute in any way to the economy of the household, was beyond their means. But Annie, the daughter born on July 28 1905 with a badly twisted left leg and a right arm she could not raise, was as loved and cared for as were her brother and sisters.

Number six, Pitt's Square, Lea Brook, Wednesbury, home to the Price family, stood at the end of a long street of terraced houses backing on to Lea Brook Sports Ground.

A water tap stood in the communal yard, which

had a privy at the further end. This was shared by three families comprising some two dozen people, a number which in later years would increase significantly as more children and grandchildren were born.

Many houses such as this set in squares or folds had in addition to share a wash-house, or, as still locally named, a 'brew 'ouse'. Number six did not: it carried the dubious privilege of a large brick-built boiler in the kitchen, and as a result wash days added to the damp of old brickwork.

This, then, was the environment into which my mother was born and where she would live the next twenty-eight years of her life.

Christened in the church of St James, Annie did not join the school of that same name at the usual age of three years, her mother perhaps fearing for the well-being of her crippled child among boisterous youngsters.

The birth of a fourth child, however, added to Mary Ann's burden of helping to support a family of three daughters and a son, none of whom were yet of an age to bring in a weekly wage. In those days, a growing family did not go hand in hand with growing weekly earnings of the father. So caring for a crippled five-year-old and a newborn baby had to be combined with Mary Ann's mode of earning a living. With children in an old pram and a bundle on her head she continued to collect clothing no longer wanted by the wealthier of Wednesbury's industrial élite, passing them on to a second-hand clothes dealer who ran a stall in Birmingham's 'Rag' market and who paid a few pence for each item.

But even the members of a coal baron's family or those wives of wealthy steel merchants could not throw out clothes willy-nilly; many days were spent picking coal from colliery waste heaps. This practice was not without hazard. Much as the material they picked was waste from the coal mines and of no value to the pit owners, those owners did not look kindly on women desperate enough to spend hours on their knees scratching among the dirt in search of tiny pieces of coal. Magistrates were informed and sometimes these 'pit bank wenches' had to endure not only a fine but also a term of imprisonment that took no regard of any children they might be forced to leave.

Weather had little effect upon the coal picking; rain, sleet, bitter winds – women and young children were forced to work through them all or go without food. Only when the heaps became frost bound and the women's fingers almost immovable due to the cold were the banks deserted.

Towards the end of the day came the Jagger. With horse-drawn cart he would visit every pit heap in turn, paying no more than sixpence however large the bag of coal a woman might have picked – often the payment was less. Protests were in vain; the threat to inform the colliery owner of their activities was more than enough to silence women's dissent, for they knew full well the measure of the man who took the proceeds of a day's work then sold it on for half again what he paid to them; they knew avarice was the foundation of his business and spite would keep it firm.

This, then, was an accepted part of Mary Ann's life. Until one particular day.

Phoebe, her youngest child, was teething. Pain kept the infant from sleeping and consequently Mary Ann also suffered a series of broken nights, but weary as this left her the day's work must be done.

Leaving her bucket every half hour to soothe the wailing Phoebe, or to lift the crippled Annie from the pram so the needs of nature could be attended to, then to breast-feed one and give a piece of bread and cheese to the other, Mary Ann found her day more fraught and less productive than usual.

This latter was remarked upon by the Jagger. Looking at a bag holding some three quarters of its more usual amount he obviously saw the chance for a larger profit than he normally made; the woman had children to keep, she would sell and be glad of the chance.

Kicking one boot against the side of the rough sack he snorted, ' 'Alf a bag be of no use to me.'

'Ain't 'alf a bag,' Mary Ann responded quickly. 'It be nigh on three quarter an' none o' it be bats, you don't find no rubbish in the bag Mary Ann Price picks!'

That was one claim the Jagger could not refute, the women he bought from knew better than to try to foist slate upon him, do it once and they wouldn't pick the bank again; but the claim of a three-quarter-filled sack he could defeat.

'Nigh on!' He kicked the sack again. 'Nigh on three quarter you says! D'ya tek me forra fool? The bag be no more than 'alf, an' that as I've said already be of no use to me, but . . .' He paused, sending a glance to the pram with its crying infant, 'I tell ya what I'll do, I'll gie ya tuppence.'

A day of constant grubbing among coal dust caked to sludge by drizzling rain added to Mary Ann's weariness from sleepless nights.

'Tuppence!' she exploded. 'You don't be satisfied with tekin' the shimmy [vest] from a baby's back, you'd tek the bread from its mouth!'

Unused to such defiance, the Jagger kicked again at the sack, the force of his foot sending it over and spilling the hard-won coal. 'I said tuppence an' tuppence it be or naught.'

'Then it be naught!' Tiredness cleared the way for Mary Ann's anger.

Aware of the other women watching, aware also

that to allow one picker to get away with defying him might well open the floodgates to the rest doing the same, the Jagger's whip hand came into play.

Loud and dominant, his voice reached over the black wastes of pit heaps. 'You refuses the money I offers, that be your choice; now 'ear the one that be mine. Tomorrow I goes to see Mister Wilson Lloyd who you all knows be the proprietor o' Forge Pool Colliery an' the owner o' this 'ere ground. 'E will be interested in my informin' him o' the pilferin' you women does, the stealin' o' coal from his property, an' learn o' it he will lessen that there bag be sold to me for the price I named.'

To do as he threatened would mean women losing what might be the only way they had of helping support a family. The poor wages earned by menfolk working in the mines or the iron and steel could not do that alone. Mary Ann realised this but she also realised she was being cheated more than ever and her Irish temper rose.

'You'll be informin' Mister Wilson Lloyd will ye? Then inform him o' this as well . . .'

The words hardly free of her mouth, she swung a tight clenched fist hard against the Jagger's face sending him sprawling in the black sludge.

'. . . an' while ye be along o' Park Lane 'Ouse be sure to inform the owner o' Forge Pool Colliery it were a woman gied ye a bloody nose . . . and 'er be ready to do it again, ye robbing bugger!'

The temper of Mary Ann, inherited from a grand-father who had come from Ireland around 1850 to work digging canals, was a byword in Pitt's Square. Few, man or woman, crossed her and those who tried came out of it the worst. Not to mention Mary Ann's husband.

The Jagger knew the strength and temper of her husband. William Henry Price was not one to stand by while his wife was threatened; though a carter and thus away from home days at a stretch he always returned, and any man who had offended Mary Ann would be paid with broken bones. Scrabbling to his feet he left, more muttered threats floating behind him.

'Ya think 'e'll tell on we, Mary Ann?'

As the women helped retrieve every last tiny jet-black kibble, returning it to the sack, they voiced their nervousness.

She could not answer. In truth, who could say what a man such as that one, a man shamed by a woman's blow and one delivered in front of a bevy of others, would do in revenge?

'I don't 'ave the answerin' o' that.' Mary Ann hoisted the sack onto her head, steadying it with one hand as she stared after the departing Jagger. 'But this much I does say . . .' her voice rose, carrying after the man, 'and Enoch Birks knows it to be no lie. So sure he speaks one word to 'im who lives along o' Park Lane then the next time he be seen it won't be leadin' no 'orse. It'll be floatin' arse up in the cut and not a whole bone in his body!'

He had not needed to hear the warning to know he must abide by it. Mary Ann and her neighbours were not brought before the Magistrate.

With Phoebe reaching the toddler stage and becoming less happy to sit hours in a pram too small to hold a pair of growing children, Mary Ann was at last forced to consider sending Annie to school. For there was no help to be got from the Council nor from the government in London. Every hard-pressed mother in Wednesbury could quote the saying by which their families' lives were led: 'If you don't work you don't eat!' It was the truth.

The sack of coal bits she knew would have to find another Jagger steadied with one hand, the other wheeling the pushchair, Mary Ann turned for home. The only help was the workhouse along Meeting Street – and they helped folk into the grave! The only answer was the first one; she would have to send Annie to school. But how would she fare? She had not the learning of those children who had the benefit of being a student some five years and more; would that mean her child would be teased, possibly laughed at?

But all these thoughts had to be put aside. Dressed in a white frilled pinafore over a blue frock, white ribbons tied to the end of two long plaits, her boots polished so they gleamed blacker than the coal Mary Ann picked, Annie was taken to St James' Church of England School.

As it happened, Mary Ann need not have feared. Clara, her older daughter, was on hand to 'persuade' the less well-intentioned child that it might be in his or her best interests not to tease her sister. The headmistress Miss Budd also took Annie beneath a benevolent wing. Several times each day she would withdraw her from lessons and taking her into her private room would remove the clumsy boot and irons supporting Annie's leg and proceed to spend an hour or so talking to her while massaging both leg and arm. This may not have added to Annie's education but it certainly prevented further deterioration of muscle as well as helping in getting a child to walk with confidence and so lead a life happily mixing with her peers. A life which at the age of twenty years was joined to that of George Henry Astbury.

On a Sunday afternoon stroll in Wednesbury's Brunswick Park, Annie and her sister Phoebe paused to listen to the town band playing in the bandstand. A young man neatly dressed in brown suit, collar and tie – everyone donned their Sunday best for this weekly

saunter – smiled politely, wishing them good afternoon.

A casual encounter, but one which over the weeks
became a regular occurrence: a smile, a few words,
pleasant moments listening to the band. But the
weeks had wrought a change. It was no longer the
music that drew George and Annie to the park, the
couple's interest was in each other. They were in love.
Fine, except that twenty-two-year-old George was
engaged to another girl.

This came as a bitter blow for seventeen-year-old
Annie. Her world had become filled with dreams,
now suddenly those dreams were shattered. They
both knew that their meetings – no longer chaper-
oned by Phoebe – should have ended then, but
neither had the emotional strength that was required
to do it.

Over eighty years ago, breaking an engagement
was not viewed with the same tolerance as it is today.
Promises given were promises to be kept. But marriage to a person you did not love could ruin more
than one life. Coming to terms with the truth of this,
George ended his engagement and two years later, on
June 28 1925, he married Annie in the church of St
James, Wednesbury, and went to live in Annie's
parents' house in Pitt's Square.

This was not the easiest of situations. William
Henry had not taken kindly to the man who had

seduced his daughter, an attitude he seemingly retained for the rest of his life.

Maybe it was the matter of Annie's father's disapproval of George, and the reason of it, that kept the story of their first meeting shrouded in mystery.

3

A Christmas Gift

On December 21 1925, Annie was in labour with her first child.

George listened while Mary Ann told her daughter 'everythin' be as it should', but each step of the way from Lea Brook to the White Horse, where they could get the tram to West Bromwich, was filled with worry. What if Mary Ann were wrong? What if everything didn't be as it should?

The jolting of the tram made Annie moan softly, the constant stopping and re-starting painting lines of anxiety over George's face.

There were no ambulances like those he had seen during the 1914–18 war, there was no help of that kind for folk who didn't have the money to pay. Should a doctor be needed he had to be paid, but that was a luxury that not many folk in Wednesbury could afford. A woman in labour, a man injured at his work, a child brought down with sickness, all were nursed by their family. It was precious few who could pay a penny a week to a hospital fund providing insurance for medical treatment. Those poor souls were forced to apply to the Poor Law and were subjected to the means test which demanded that everything a body had that could be sold was sold before they were given a farthing. Thank God George had a job and was able to pay that penny, and so did not have to apply to the Poor Law to provide for Annie's delivery.

The journey seemed unending, the time it was taking appeared ten times longer than usual! George fretted, his lips white and set.

Hallam Hospital was a grim-looking brick-built Victorian edifice, its dark covering of soot from countless factory smoke stacks adding to its forbidding exterior. But here were the doctors and nurses who could help his wife. Holding to this thought, George answered the questions of a thin-faced woman at the reception desk.

'What name is the patient? Patient's age? Has the patient visited the hospital before today? Name of patient's doctor?'

They went on until George wanted to shake the woman, to shout couldn't she see his wife was in pain!

Sensing his distress above her own, Annie slipped her hand into his. 'It'll be all right,' she murmured, 'it'll be over soon.'

But soon could not be soon enough. Half carrying

Annie in the direction pointed by the thin-faced receptionist, George lived a lifetime in every moment.

'You can go home now!' Crisp as her starched apron, the folds of an equally starched cap touching her shoulders, a nurse barred the way into the maternity unit.

'Visiting is allowed Wednesdays and Sundays, three o' clock until four.'

That was all. No smile, no reassurance, just a polite way of saying 'sling your hook'. George stared at the door which had closed on Annie and that starch-tongued nurse. He couldn't go home, he couldn't leave Annie here alone. But the next steps along the high-ceilinged, brown and yellowed-cream-painted corridor were those of a porter. Though more sympathetic the man was adamant. George must leave.

Christmas Eve. Annie glanced about the maternity ward empty except for herself. Hilda May, born in the small hours of December 22, had arrived safely and with mother and child both doing well, just one nurse was on duty in the ward, the others having been granted a couple of hours off in order that they might exchange gifts and greetings in another part of the building. Saddened by the young nurse's obvious disappointment, Annie urged her to 'forget duty for a few minutes and look in' on the gathering. After all, the baby was in a cot beside the bed, they were both perfectly all right. 'What harm could come of a few minutes?'

Uncertainty flickered over the face of the nurse; dare she risk Ward Sister or worse, Matron, discovering such an escapade? But it was Christmas Eve, and she would be gone only for a moment.

Temptation, aided and abetted by Annie's encouraging smile, overcame resistance. But before scampering off for her stolen moment the nurse first brought a large Alsatian dog to lie beside Annie's bed.

Questions as to the reason of this would eat away the promised minutes, but the exit of her smiling nurse left Annie feeling apprehensive. Was it the usual thing to do? Why bring a dog into the ward? Why such a big dog?

Questions need answers and seconds after the quick tap of the nurse's footsteps had faded the answers were given.

From the floor a soft growl played on the silence. Annie looked at the dog. Hair bristling, teeth bared, it growled a second time.

What had disturbed it? Why was it growling?

Wishing she had not urged the nurse to leave, Annie clutched the sheet with trembling fingers. Then she heard it, a sound like the scrabbling of fingernails against a board and with it a soft high-pitched laugh. The dog bounded across the room and rose on its hind legs, snarling at a heavy door inset with a small iron grille and behind the grille was the grinning face of a man.

The maternity unit adjoined the Borough Asylum for the mentally disturbed, one of whose number Annie would declare for the rest of her life had called and grinned at her until the return of the nurse chased him away.

As was the custom in Pitt's Square, Annie's child was welcomed with a smile, nobody having money to spare for gifts, and the clothes it wore were necessarily of the second-time-around variety. Lodgings in her parents' home provided a roof over the head but paying rent, plus buying coal for a fire and oil for the lamps bit deeply into the nineteen shillings weekly wage George earned at the nearby Victoria Iron Works. But at least her husband had a job, Annie comforted herself, not like many poor souls in Wednesbury now so many of the coal pits had closed their gates. It wasn't easy, and often dinner was no more than a stew made of scrag end of mutton and a few carrots and parsnips she could set on the table when George came home at night, but thank God they had a meal.

Then George became one of the 'poor souls'.

Demand for iron fell by the month, workers had to be laid off, George became unemployed.

Wednesbury had more than one iron works, so

George reassured her, but as days spent trying each foundry in turn asking for employment proved, these too were laying their workers off.

A few days here, a day or two there, gladly doing any job that would bring a few pence, George trudged the town looking for work while in their single room Annie fretted. She had one child a little over a year old and was pregnant with a second. How would they live? How could she stretch a penny to do the work of a shilling?

Mary Ann had lived these times before and now she would live them again alongside her daughter. 'Life be like a penny dip,' she answered the distraught Annie, 'sometimes it tastes sweet and brings a smile, at others it be bitter and brings no pleasure, we can only trust the good Lord to give we strength to bear whatever we draws.'

And as life would prove, Annie would need all of her strength.

Phoebe Mary, my second eldest sister, joined the family on January 10 1928 with the caul still wrapped about her. The mark of good luck, delighted nursing staff beamed, this child will have good luck all through life.

Barely two years later it seemed the luck had already run out. Phoebe Mary was suddenly fever-ish. Through the next night and the next a worried

Annie and George took turns sitting beside their sick daughter.

'It be no more than the teethin'.' Grandmother Mary Ann Price put the whole thing in simple terms. 'That babby be getting' 'er back teeth and they always gives trouble, you should know that what with 'avin' one babby afore this'n. Stop yer frettin', her'll be all right once them teeth be through!'

Calling in each day to see if the infant were better the older women of Pitt's Square reinforced Mary Ann's opinion. 'Teethin' always knocks babbies about, but they gets over it.'

Annie knew this too, hadn't her firstborn cried from the pain? Rubbing a maternal finger over enflamed gums had soothed Hilda but no amount of the same treatment was giving relief to Phoebe, who didn't even cry but simply lay limp and un-moving.

Consultation between Mary Ann and neighbours resulted in the revised opinion: this was not the usual teething problem. That resolved, the 'cures' were brought.

'Give 'er a few drops o' this, me wench, it be good for fever.' Mrs Butler produced a bottle of home-made Surfeit Water – a teaspoon of fine ash taken from the grate, mixed with water from the pump and warmed over the fire.

'A teaspoon o' this in a drop o' water.' Mrs Walker

advised Ipecachuana Wine. It would have Phoebe well in no time.

But neither the Surfeit Water nor the Ipecachuana Wine brought the promised improvements, neither did the blackcurrant cordial Mrs Griffiths had made by pouring boiling water into the empty jam pot and swirling it around to dissolve those last remnants of jam neither spoon nor knife could entirely scrape up. Though each in turn was tried, Phoebe did not respond.

All of this was kindness and Annie respected it, thanking them for their words as she did for their medicines. It was Mrs Hogan who suggested two pennyworth of brandy be fetched from the nearby Boat Inn. Added to hot water sweetened with sugar this would 'warm the belly an' 'elp the circilashun'. It had, she assured Annie, 'never bin a known to fail, the babby would a start gettin' well afore cock crow.'

The brandy duly fetched and diluted as instructed, black-skirted women sat like a flock of crows on the scrubbed wooden squab waiting to see the promised cure.

Oblivious of the drama taking place inside the house the four-year-old Hilda turned a contemptu-ous back on Tea Leaves, the donkey kept in a stable at the bottom of the yard. Maybe Grandma would have a toffee. Today Mary Ann had no time to find a sweet, but the cup on the table looked interesting.

The women's attention on the child Annie was nursing, no one noticed Hilda. Not until the contents of the 'pretty cup' had her choking for breath.

For Mary Ann, one grandchild choking, the other looking as if the Angel of Death were already gathering her into his arms, was too much. Fastening her black bonnet, then donning the shawl she reached from a peg behind the kitchen door, she ushered the women from the house. What she intended was not for their knowing.

Sitting Hilda in the pushchair, she hurried along Dudley Street. She had never asked for charity and she was not about to ask it now.

Reaching the junction with Holyhead Road, she turned left. This was the way she had brought her own children to school, but it was not the school she was visiting today.

'I wants the lending of 'alf a crown!' Firm in her resolve Mary Ann's stare held the crafty eyes watching her over the pawnshop counter. 'It be gold through and through an' it be heavy; you knows the value of it, George Jones, so don't you be a'wastin' my time pretendin' it 'as no worth.'

'Two shillin' and sixpence be a lot o' money.' Round-shouldered from stooping long hours over the counter of his gloomily lighted shop, the pawnbroker hesitated.

'That which you be 'oldin' in your 'and be worth

several times that, but I don't be goin' to stand arguin'!'

His hand closing over the wedding ring Mary Ann made to retrieve from his palm, the pawnbroker nodded then proceeded to write the date and amount loaned on a small white ticket. Three months his customer had to reclaim her pledge. Chances were it would never be used to redeem the ring.

The transaction finished, the silver coin in the pocket of her vast black skirt, Mary Ann next stopped at number one Loxdale Street, the house of Edward Alfred Dingley. As Poor Law medical officer he could have been requested to examine the sick child, and be paid by the Parish, but as long as the good Lord provided any other means Mary Ann would take naught from the Parish.

A home visit by the doctor plus a bottle of medicine would account for almost all of the half crown. What if a second visit were required? Pushing the thought to the back of her mind, Mary Ann grasped the gleaming brass doorknocker. She would cross that bridge when she came to it.

The child was suffering from pneumonia. Edward Dingley looked with sympathy at Annie. It was too far advanced for any hope of a recovery; she must be brave. Then he murmured to Mary Ann, 'The child will not live until morning.'

Annie sat stunned. The child she loved was to be

taken from her! Her laughing, into-everything scamp of a daughter was dying. All afternoon she held the precious bundle close against her breast unwilling to part with it a single second before she must. The Lord's Will be done, that was the teaching of Church. Eyes closed against tears choking every word she whispered, 'Please, please, Lord, let my child live, don't take her from me.'

The last sob was drowned by a braying from the yard. In Annie's arms the child stirred, opened her eyes and said, 'That's Tea Leaves, he wants his dinner.'

Phoebe survived pneumonia. The good luck that goes with being born in a caul? Annie never thought so. Yet with the passing years George would come to say of his second born, 'Should that one tumble off the Town Hall roof her'd land on a mattress!'

4

Another Debut

Life in Pitt's Square flitted like shadows from one dark patch to an even darker one. Employment was so hard to find and could be – and often was – ended with a word. No Union protection meant a man being subject to the whim of his boss. Being sacked resulted in 'going on the Labour'.

Social Security of the time held none of the backup of today. Uncovenanted Benefit (dole) consisted of no more than the barest minimum allowance. In the case of George, with a wife and now three children as dependents, this benefit consisted of a weekly payment of seventeen shillings. No rent rebate, no attendance or disability allowance, in short no consideration of hardship of any kind was taken into account; payment was given grudgingly, many contributors to the Poor Law system viewing applicants as scroungers.

Stretching that sum into clothing, feeding and keeping a roof over their head meant folk considering every farthing a dozen times before spending it.

Means-tested support had new clothing rarer than jewels in the King's crown, so Annie's children, like those of other families whose father was unemployed, never got to experience that delight. Dresses already second-hand when bought from jumble sales or made from bits and pieces that Mary Ann sometimes took in exchange for a few bits of coal picked from pit waste heaps passed from Hilda to Phoebe and, when they became too small for her, were passed to other mothers with younger, smaller children. Just once, at Christmas time, would the Poor Law issue a voucher for 'one article of footwear'. Using that to purchase shoes for a child was unthinkable when it could provide boots for a man tramping every day in search of work.

But one extravagance George did indulge in. Collecting his 'labour pay' once a week, he would visit the Shambles to buy a pound of sausages. A pound of sausages – one link for each person and served with boiled potatoes – provided several meals.

It was to the Shambles -- the section of the street market in which butchers had their stalls – that women would go each Saturday night in hope of a bargain. A regular jug of ale from the nearby Green Dragon or Turk's Head had one or two butchers turn the final couple of hours of trading into something of an auction. This practice proved a magnet for Wednesbury's less than wealthy.

Summer and winter, no matter how cold or wet the weather, they would stand patiently waiting, ever hopeful the next 'lot' to be offered might prove one they could afford.

Every woman in the Square knew of this practice of selling cheaply the meat remaining from the day's trading rather than holding it over to another week. Consequently Saturday late evening became a prime time to shop for a weekend joint or a piece for the stew jar. Annie and her mother were no exception. But careful as she was, try as she might, the 'Benefit' allowance never lasted as long as the week. Half of the house rent, gas for cooking and oil for the lamp plus coal and the cost of other household necessities such as disinfectant, a must for cleaning the communal toilet and used in the constant struggle against vermin, left little for food and less for clothes and shoes.

December 1930 had fastened a hard grip on the pit heaps where many folk picked coal despite its practice being against the law. But with the freezing of the ground this became impossible. Buying from a coal merchant or from a Jagger would take a hefty slice of her housekeeping, but Annie knew it was buy coal or risk her family going down with pneumonia, in that ever-present threat of damp, cold housing.

But a hot meal, that was needed too by George and the children as for herself she could manage on a slice of bread.

Hearing her mother call from the next room, Annie again checked the coppers in her purse even though she knew every coin by heart. One shilling and six pennies to see a family of five until the next 'dole' payment, another six days. Should she even be thinking of luxuries such as meat?

Mary Ann too had pondered that same problem. Like her daughter she also must provide out of very little. But the Lord was good. Bonnet in place, shawl tied corner to corner beneath her breasts she called again to Annie. They had to go now if they hoped to get any meat at all.

Swallowing the tears itching in her throat, Annie looked at her children, the youngest in the pushchair, her eldest, buttoned in the warmest clothes a jumble sale had provided, standing beside it. Maybe the money could stretch to a bit of neck end or a few pork bones, either would make a nourishing broth.

Wednesbury market stalls stood in the main thoroughfare from 1709 until 1970 when they were moved to covered premises on the site of Camphill Lane. To the left, beneath the sign 'Butlers' can be seen the first stalls of the Shambles.

In 1824, where the present-day clock stands on the site of the ancient Butter Cross, Moses Maggs, known locally as Rough Moey, sold his wife Sally and their child for the sum of six shillings.

Strung about with gas lamps, the market stalls lent

the darkness a fairytale setting. Glittering and gleaming, they held for Hilda, the four-year-old clutching her grandmother's voluminous black skirts, the promise of dreams.

Clothing new or second-hand, shoes boasting of scarcely any previous wear, pots, pans, crockery – all was for sale in a magic arena alive with sounds. Competing with the rattle of a tram, Maggie O'Connell proclaimed her fruit and vegetables; competing yet not quite winning the shouting match, Edward Tedd called the value of a 'nice bit o'cod . . . a couple o' herring', or 'this be the best place for plaice', the smell of wet fish carrying on the air almost as far as his voice. A step away the aroma of chestnuts and potatoes roasting on a hand-propelled cart vied with that of Purslow's freshly cooked pork pies and the deliciously inviting smell of Hickinbottom's bread; but holding tightly to her grandmother's skirts, Hilda had eyes for only one stall.

Teddy Gray sold every type of sweet. Dark brown Brandy Balls, striped Humbugs, black Liquorice Shoelaces, bright red Cherry Lips, pink and white Sugared Almonds, the whole stall was a panorama of delights, a veritable paradise for the child gazing longingly at it. Mother and Grandmother always spent a minute here talking with the stallholder and buying a happorth of Palm Toffee for her and a

happorth of something each for Phoebe and Ann. But
tonight Annie and her mother walked on past the
wonderful stall: money for such a treat could not be
spared.

'Who'll gie me a shillin' for this . . .? A tanner for
half a pig's 'ead . . . ninepence for a bit o'
topside . . .'

Calls from various butchers' stalls echoed along the
Shambles. Standing among the crowd, all waiting for
the one offer they could afford to take, Annie worried
for her children beginning to whimper against the
cold bite of frost.

It was useless, there would be no meat cheap
enough to justify spending her last shilling. Mary
Ann and Annie turned away; bread toasted before
the fire would be the only warm meal for yet another
day.

'Hey up, mah babby!' A hand reached to the
child now clinging to the handle of the pushchair,
'. . . What be yoh'r name?'

'Hilda.' The reply came on lips trembling with the
disappointment of being bought no toffee. 'My name
is Hilda.'

'Hilda be it!' Mr Poxon at the poultry stall smiled
down at the small girl. 'Well, Hilda wench, tek this
and tell yoh'r mother to cook it.'

A laugh gurgling up from his stomach, he placed a
plump chicken in her arms.

Desperately fighting her tears of gratitude, Annie took her daughters to Teddy Gray's stall. She would spend those halfpennies and worry over it later.

Despite the constant struggle to make ends meet and the hardship and worry of wartime, growing up in the Black Country was not all doom and gloom.

Before that conflict began, Wednesbury, as did so many towns, held its yearly carnival. Annie took a special delight in these and, despite her handicap, would make costumes for Hilda and Phoebe so they could take part in the grand parade. This was always followed by a competition for the 'best' or most creative entry.

At two years old and still recovering from pneumonia Phoebe was unable to walk the route through the town, so dressed as a doll, her pushchair bedecked in ribbons and lace, she was wheeled along. So appealing did she look in blue bonnet and frilly dress that oohs and aahs followed the pushchair and the 'baby doll' won the competition.

Was it a memory of this a year or so later had Phoebe 'dress' a tiny piglet in bonnet and shawl only to wheel it about the yard of number six Pitt Square in an ancient pram declaring it her 'dolly'?

Pre-war years also witnessed Sunday School outings. One of these was an excursion to Sutton Park. That was thrilling in itself, but the journey was to be made by train; for two little girls, neither of whom had ever been on a train, this was pure heaven.

Their faces scrubbed pink, dressed in the frocks kept for Sunday church, eight-year-old Hilda and six-year-old Phoebe were taken to the L.M.S. railway station to begin their 'Alice in Wonderland' adventure.

The day went well. They had enjoyed every moment, they told Father who, knowing they would be tired after the excitement of the day, had taken the pushchair to greet their return to the railway station.

But the day had one more event in store. Phoebe was sitting on Hilda's lap and they were almost home when, just before the junction of Holyhead Road and Dangerfield Lane, a motor vehicle – something of a rarity in those days – caught an animal in its headlights. The rabbit, so it proved, mesmerised by the lights, was run over, the vehicle rolling on regardless.

But the rabbit was not disregarded for long. A quick dash onto the roadway and it was in Father's hands. Carrying it home he presented it to Mother. Next day the family sat down to a meal of rabbit stew.

Eked out by pearl barley and several additions of water the rabbit stew was made to feed Father, Mother and three kids until the next payment from the Assistance Board became due. Once this handout was spent there would be nothing more no matter the circumstances; that was the raw fact of life for the unemployed and the reason caution was repeated each time a youngster was sent on an errand.

The confined space of that one room became more restricted when, on October 6 1930 my third sister, Ann Georgina, was added to the family. The strain of making the paltry Benefit Allowance last the week did not make itself felt in the months the child could be breast-fed. But the clothes – not new in the first place – had been made to serve two children before and were beyond wearing again, so more must need be bought.

Life was indeed hard for Annie. Nor was it less stressful for George living in the house of a father-in-law who had never approved of him. For William Henry, the fact that his daughter had been seduced was a craw that stuck in his throat.

Having run away to join the army at fourteen years of age, spending years in India, becoming a sergeant major there before returning to civilian life, William Henry had little time for shirkers, and in his eyes George was a shirker.

Mary Ann, though, was more in touch with the realities of life. William Henry was a carter and that meant his often being away from home. He did not know the hours that their daughter's husband trekked the town looking for work nor did he see the exhaustion when he returned, often too tired to eat; but she saw, she knew and respected George and he in turn loved Mary Ann.

George, ever a gentle person, worried whenever the sounds of argument issued from his parents-in-law's part of the house. His fiery, five foot nothing mother-in-law could hold her own with any woman in Pitt's Square and their husbands too if need be, but she was less of a match for William Henry, who was six foot four and powerfully built.

Hearing her cry, George ran into their living room, to see William Henry with his hand raised, about to hit Mary Ann. George struck first, landing him a blow to the head. Enraged, William Henry made to strike back but George grabbed his wrist. William Henry sank his teeth into the hand restraining his, almost severing the tip of George's little finger, releasing it only when a second blow knocked him away.

Even though his pride was more offended than his body injured, William Henry issued George with his marching orders: he should leave the house that minute.

Three children, one of them just a few months old, and now homeless. Annie was heartbroken but determined. If George went, so did she and the children. Taking no account of George begging her to remain, she woke the two older children and dressed them in the warmest clothes they had. With the baby in George's arms, they left.

Given lodgings with Charlie 'Buller' Norton and his wife, people who would prove to be lifelong friends, they were squeezed into a tiny, already crowded house, staying there until a grudging William Henry agreed to their returning to number six. From that time until he died thirty years later, William Henry never spoke another word to his son-in-law.

Life, which had never been easy, was not improved by this family upset.

The installation of a gas cooker was something of an improvement on the previous method of cooking over the open fire, or in the oven which was part of the black cast-iron firegrate. But this luxury did not compensate for or help in the struggle against damp and rotting woodwork. A struggle made the harder with a fourth pregnancy.

Wearied by long hours of labour, exhausted from the pain of giving birth, Annie felt the sharp sting of disappointment add to her tears. Another daughter! She had been so sure this time, so certain the good Lord would send the longed-for son, the boy she and George, her husband, dreamed of having.

But Heaven had not listened to her prayers. Annie blinked warm tears onto her cheeks. It had denied her that one wish, a son to carry on her husband's name. She looked at the child lying asleep in her arms.

Another girl – the fourth in a row! Well, Heaven could take back its daughter!

Quick as the thought, she pushed the tiny blanket-wrapped bundle beneath the covers of the bed. She wouldn't take another one home, she wouldn't!

Born in Hallam Hospital maternity unit on July 16 1933, this was the first taste of life for Margaret Rose, the child Annie snatched back into her arms to cover with fresh tears; the child she would love and cherish as she did the rest of her brood.

What a disappointment I must have been!

5

Some Things Change

There can be no doubting that a fourth daughter was initially a disappointment for my mother. Where was the son her nightly prayers had asked for, where was the boy she had longed to place in her husband's arms? But Father showed not the least regret: he adored his little 'Rosie' as he adored his other three girls. To him, each of his children was a direct gift from heaven and every moment which offered itself he would spend with us, making up games, walking with us along the canalside or in the park, always explaining, always pointing out, never brushing aside a question.

If bad weather barred these activities, then he would have an impromptu music hall show. Father could dance tap, black bottom and do a mean soft shoe shuffle. He would sing the popular tunes of the day while teaching Hilda and Phoebe these dances, but dancing with Father wasn't enough for Phoebe; ever the exhibitionist, she liked a solo spot. 'Sing, Dad,' she would say, 'sing "When the little red robin comes bob, bob, bobbing along".' Always happy to oblige, he would sing and she would perform a tap routine. One other favourite song, as each child came along, was adapted to include their name, all of us squeaking our delight when given the 'star' spot of beating the drum. As I remember, the words were:

Little Hilda Morgan played the organ,
Phoebe beat the drum,
Ann, she played on the tambourine,
And Margaret went boom, boom, boom, boom,
    boom.

Encores of this would be called for over and over, the names rotating to keep everybody happy, but still we would ask, 'Dad, can I play the drum this time?' The drum? That was totally imaginary, it was just Dad clapping his hands on his knees, providing the rhythm, but for us kids it was an orchestra.

Dancing each of us around the room in turn – my just being a few months old, I was carried in his arms – required an interval for him to catch his breath. This part of the entertainment would see each of us do our party piece, either a song, a poem or, as always with Phoebe, a dance.

Mother would often shake her head and say, 'Her's got St Vitus dance!' but there was always a note of pride in the saying. Phoebe was forever 'jigging', dancing to every note of music she might hear, and often when she heard none at all. We have all grown up loving to dance, but she most of all.

Then there were times when Father would say, 'I've got a little conundrum for you.' There were many of these brain teasers. This one left us all wondering:

> Riddle me, riddle me, rote-te-tote,
> I met a man in a red coat,
> A stick in his hand,
> And a stone in his throat,
> Riddle me, riddle me, rote-te-tote.

Begged to give the answer, Father would simply repeat the riddle. How frustrated we all got! Finally, Mother put us out of our misery. The man in a red coat was a cherry.

It was not only riddles we were set to puzzle over. He would pose questions our young minds found quite daunting. He always began by saying, 'I've got one for you.'

'George!' Mother would frown. 'Remember they're only babbies!'

That didn't stop Father! He would chuckle, then still ask the question. A regular one was, 'How many beans make five?'

We never quite got the answer, for the simple reason he changed it every time!

'Two beans and half a bean, two beans and a half',

'A bean, a bean and half a bean, a bean, a bean and a half', 'Half a bean, half a bean', and so on. How could there be so many ways of coming up with five? It was an early lesson in the use of fractions.

I often wonder at the patience both Mother and Father showed playing with us, keeping us happy while they worried over unemployment, or sharing someone else's house and backyard privy. It was with the borough embarking upon a slum clearance scheme, replacing condemned houses with new buildings, that things changed for the better, at least as far as living conditions were concerned. Pitt's Square was to be demolished and in May 1934 my parents were given a brand new council house.

At last they were to have a home of their own, a place free of mice, 'blackbats' (beetles) and other unwelcome residents of the houses of Pitt's Square.

Annie wept tears of joy when she received notification of rehousing. She would take her three older children to school and then with ten-month-old Margaret Rose in the battered old pram which had served many a child before being acquired by Annie eight years before and used daily ever since, would go to the Council housing department there to collect the keys to the newly constructed Number 51 Dangerfield Lane.

Standing alone, the first of the few in every sense of the word, it stood in what is today a street of some length with houses lining both sides. But in May of 1934 it had only half-erected buildings as neighbours. No surfaced road led to Annie's dream. Helped by her sister Clara, she pushed the pram over mud-hardened ruts carved deep by wagons and carts. Seeing them approach a kindly builder laid a plank of wood across the mud to rest upon the step giving onto the front door of the house.

No red carpet could have been more wonderful. No king and Queen entering their royal palace could have experienced more delight and happiness than Annie as she stepped for that first time into her very own home.

A house of their own. No more sharing one room. The worries that came with the stress of living in such close, confined quarters, the fear of upsetting Annie's father.

William Henry never forgave his son-in-law and was never once to set foot in the house in Dangerfield Lane.

Mary Ann took a different view. True, her girl had been wronged but unlike many another who had fallen pregnant before wedlock she had not been left to face the music alone. The man had married her, had taken on his responsibilities; William Henry's grandchildren had not entered this world as bastards.

With this in mind Mary Ann happily set to helping pile the few bits and pieces of furniture spared from her own home onto the handcart George had borrowed in order to transport them to Dangerfield Lane.

Bliss for him? Definitely. Relief for Annie? Assuredly. But though life in their new home meant a sister sharing a bedroom with only one sister, a large garden space front and rear, life for the children continued much as before . . . up to the armpits in mischief!

New home, the end of old differences? Not for William Henry. Though Mary Ann, her daughter and son-in-law stayed close, William Henry remained obstinately silent and unforgiving. Though he was not above having his hair cut regularly by this same son-in-law!

Hilda, named after that same young nurse who had left the Alsatian guarding Mother's bedside, was the eldest of Mother's children and probably the most sensible, but even she was not above a little mischief.

The houses of Pitt's Square and its surrounding environs of back-to-back buildings had long been condemned. One by one families were slowly rehoused, the resultant empty buildings boarded up prior to demolition.

Such a house was number 110. Vacant and mysterious, it beckoned Hilda and her friend Nellie Walker. They would investigate. At eight years old, such an undertaking was a great adventure. Entering the silent deserted house via a ground-floor window they found partly free of board, clutching each other's hands as trails of delicious excitement raced along their spines, the girls proceeded to explore the gloomy emptiness. Except the house was not empty.

Delighted with the sound of their shoes tapping on bare wooden flooring, they giggled and jumped. Banging feet even harder increased their pleasure and shouts of laughter sent echoes through the silence. But laughter quickly turned into terrified screams.

The jumping had brought a mass of fleas from decaying woodwork and plaster and soon Hilda and Nellie were covered head to foot in a cloud of biting parasites. Their cries brought rapid rescue from the house but reprieve from the bite of hundreds of fleas was small relief compared to the wrath of Mother. Having to stand in the yard, doused by bucket after bucket of water from the pump while their clothes were burned on a bonfire drowned any desire to repeat the adventure. Needless to say that one episode marked the end of Hilda's breaking and entering aspirations.

Hilda was not the only one finding mischief; her younger sister was proving equally expert.

Ann Georgina, the third child born to Annie, was a prime player when it came to doing what she shouldn't. With Hilda and Phoebe sent off to school, it was Ann's turn to be washed in the old brownstone sink. Once dressed, fine blonde hair plaited and ribboned, it was out in the yard . . . and mischief.

Ann's favourite pastime was making mud pies. Puddles of overnight rain mixed with dust and dirt scraped from any convenient corner accommodated this play very nicely, the resultant mud being gleefully plastered over hands, face and any other part of the body. Clothing proved no deterrent whatsoever; in fact it too was liberally daubed, Ann viewing the result as perfectly acceptable decoration.

You think there was a break in behaviour during dry spells?

Think again!

Ann was a determined child. She knew what she wanted and could see no reason why she should not have it, regardless of what others might think.

This was the logic behind refusing to be deprived of her beloved pie making. If there was no rain, she would simply use that other source which nature supplied. Off would come her drawers and she would wee on the ground. At three years old, this appeared a most sensible way of proceeding.

Trying unsuccessfully to cure Ann of this habit, worn out from bathing her errant toddler and washing mud-plastered clothes several times a day, Annie was at her wits end; nothing, but nothing kept Ann from her particular delight.

Eventually, salvation for Mother and retribution for child came in the shape of Mrs Hogan. She lived in a house a few doors from that of Grandmother Price, and shared still by Annie and George. A formidable woman in side button boots, long black skirts and ankle-length apron of the same colour, she was feared by all the kids in Pitt's Square. One morning the dragon, as she was called, waited for Ann to mix her piddle plaster. Then, unseen and unheard by the child intent on daubing every inch of herself in dirty grey mud, she came up behind and roared in her most fearsome voice, 'Yoh little bugger . . . I'll smack yer bloody arse fer yoh!'

The exercise in 'skin care' ended that day. No more piddle face packs, no more moisturising body creams. Antisocial Ann's pastime may have been, unhygienic it definitely was, but to this day Ann has a wrinkle-free skin and nary a blemish.

Piddle and plaster was relegated to the realms of the abandoned but mischief still had a long life to live.

6

Trials and Tribulations

Her children's early years allowed little respite from the trials and tribulations Mother had experienced while living in Pitt's Square. Each new day a few more would be added to the list.

An early one was my 'swimming' in a lime pit. Not yet old enough for school, I was playing with Georgie Bladen, a boy of about my own age. On the opposite side of the lane, another line of council houses was being erected and Father had gained temporary employment as bricklayer's labourer.

You must already be ahead! Yes, the two of us wandered onto the building site. We played happily for some time before the game of climbing a pile of bricks then jumping to the ground developed into a challenge. Who could climb higher and jump further than the other?

Denials became more heated and inevitably the first blow was struck. The nickname 'Mardy Margie' given me by my three sisters was well deserved; if I didn't get my own way I'd get annoyed and that day was no different. Rather heatedly telling Georgie he had not climbed higher than me, I pushed him. Georgie pushed back, sending me toppling into a shallow square-cut pit in the ground that was filled with quick-lime, used in the making of mortar.

My squeal must have alerted a workman who shouted to Father, 'Yoh'r babby be in the lime pit!'

I couldn't see what all the fuss was about. Father grabbed me, wiping my face on a rag before running with me in his arms the few yards to the house where Mother burst into tears, at the same time tearing my clothes away. This seemed quite unnecessary. Wasn't I always fighting with Georgie, and didn't I always win? What I did not know was that quicklime burns the skin and can cause blindness if it enters the eyes. No wonder Father rushed me home and Mother was full of tears.

Needless to say there were no more games played on that building site.

Three years after moving to Dangerfield Lane, Annie was delivered of another child, the fifth and final addition to the Astbury family, a child which brought delight, one who would be loved and cherished as were its sisters.

No, you are all wrong! The baby was yet one more girl.

November 11 1936, and as mother always dramatically described, 'At exactly eleven o' clock in the mornin', just as the bulls [sirens] was blowin' 'er was born.' ''Er' being the fifth daughter.

But whether she was delivered at the precise moment the siren commemorating the ending of the First World War was being sounded or not, she most certainly began, and continued to follow, life in the pattern of her older sisters.

The day of the christening was overhung with veils of damp grey mist, not the best of days for walking the long distance from the Lane to St James' Church, but like each of Annie's other children this one too must be baptised.

Three years earlier, the unemployment figures had reached the point where the level of benefit paid had to be reduced. As a result of this the one pound and four shillings now paid to keep Father, Mother and four children had been cut by two shillings, leaving the family struggling to exist on twenty-two shillings. Like elastic, every one of those pennies remaining after payment of six shillings and ninepence rent, had to be stretched as far as possible, and many times did not stretch to a coin for gas or electricity meters and certainly not to the amount needed for the christening party to take the Midland Red bus which passed St James' Street.

The solution was found. A three-halfpence ticket would pay for Mother and Baby to ride the bus to church and back, while Father, with Mother's sisters, Clara and Phoebe, and Grandfather William Henry filling the role of Godparents, made the same journey on foot.

Slotted between Sunday afternoon and evening services the ceremony went well enough. The priest, Father Geoffrey Ingle-Soden, holding the baby in his arms asked, 'What name is given this child?'

'Iris June,' the Godmother duly replied.

Dipping a hand into the font, Father Soden traced the sign of the cross on the tiny forehead while intoning,

> In the name of the Father,
> And of the Son,
> And of the Holy Ghost,
> I name this child . . .

And so he did, but not the chosen Iris June. Maybe the reply to his question had been somewhat lost in the echoing emptiness of the church, or maybe the loud wail the infant had chosen that same moment to give had drowned it, or even as Annie declared later, 'The vicar was deaf!' Whatever the cause, the child which had been carried into church as Iris June was carried out as Irene Joan!

The question of mishearing remains a bone of contention to this day. My sisters, Hilda, eleven years old at that time, and Phoebe, nine years old, still stoutly maintain there was dissension in the ranks. The names Irene and Joan were the same as those of the daughters of Herbert and Clara Bluck, the Clara in question being Mother's sister. Father, however, said no. Having no great liking for Clara and a downright dislike of Herbert, whom he always referred to as 'von Kluck', he did not want his little girl named after Clara's daughters.

But Mother always got her own way. Fair means or this time not so fair? Local pronunciation can, when spoken quickly, easily lead to misinterpretation on the part of a listener not attuned to Black Country dialect. Mother would be well aware of the Reverend Geoffrey Ingle-Soden's being unfamiliar with it. Did she then contrive to have him make a 'mistake'? Was that the real reason Iris June became Irene Joan?

Mother, of course, stuck to her declaration that 'the vicar was deaf'. Whether he was or not, we had a Joan.

Magnanimous in defeat, Father accepted the 'accident'. After all, what did it matter, he had pet names for each one of us anyway. Hilda was Ludy, Phoebe was Peebee, Ann somehow became Annigo, Joan was Joany Pony and me? I was Rosie Posy. Margaret or Rosie Posy, Joan or Joany Pony, we two youngest soon became versed in the family tradition, we could find mischief as skilfully and as quickly as our sisters.

Our parents' bedroom being at the front of the

house, it was lighter and larger than the others. It also held two intriguing built-in cupboards, the bigger of which was set in a rectangular alcove and so was unseen from the bedroom doorway. Allowed to play in any part of the house, one afternoon we chose 'Mom's room'. The cupboard soon beckoned. What delights might it hold, what treasures would we find? Totally immersed in this Adventure into the Unknown, we gave no heed to the cupboard door closing as we clambered inside. Curiosity being the spur, we delved among things Mother had stored against 'a time comin' when they might be wanted'. At barely six and three years old respectively, we knew nothing of oxygen, nothing of the fact that it was lack of air that was making us feel more and more sleepy.

When she got no response to her calls, Mother presumed we had gone into the garden. A glance through the window showed we were not there. Well, no need to worry, her two had gone to play with neighbours' kids and would be back soon enough.

But when 'soon enough' didn't come Mother began to feel the first twinges of irritation. 'School holidays be all well and good, but they leaves kids with the more time to find mischief.' Neighbours agreed while telling Mother they had not seen us.

Returning from their own particular afternoon pursuit, Hilda, Phoebe and Ann were told, 'Go find 'em, and if they be lost then tell 'em it be no good them come runnin' to me to find 'em!'

As with her own enquiries, this bore no fruit and Mother's irritation became concern. Dire threats were mumbled, the least of which being, so my sisters still tell, 'Their backsides will sting for a week once I gets 'old of 'em!'

It was Phoebe, going upstairs to fetch her tap-dancing shoes, who heard a faint sound from Mother's bedroom. But Phoebe wasn't going to investigate. If it should be a mouse, then let somebody else find it!

'You be 'earing things!' Already more than a little worried, Mother snapped the reply when Hilda repeated what Phoebe had whispered. But the sound had to be investigated. I can only say that, in her relief of finding her 'two little 'uns', Mother's threat of backsides being made to sting was forgotten.

Mother's bedroom, as I said, had two built-in wall cupboards. The one two inquisitive sisters got themselves locked into was fairly large and square, the other, squeezed between wall and fireplace, was narrow. Almost of a height with the ceiling, this cupboard too was inviting, especially so at Christmas time. Out would come tree ornaments and paper streamers and in would go whatever presents Mother had managed to get.

We were told where these waited for Christmas

Eve, we were even allowed to look into the cupboard. But the caution was given: open one and Christmas is cancelled. Looking back, seeing the mischievous lot we were, I wonder how the strategy worked, but work it did for not one single package was ever opened.

One Christmas delight, though, was not kept so secret. Using a cardboard box obtained from Patty Longmore's grocery shop, a doll bought for a penny from a church hall jumble sale and a packet of crepe paper, part of the treasure trove Joan and myself had rummaged among in the large cupboard, Mother produced a table ornament her daughters remember with fondness. Standing some eighteen inches high, a red crepe paper skirt spread as wide, a white bodice spangled with tiny dots of silver tinsel, a red paper-covered poke bonnet also touched with silver and a red muff, our 'crinoline lady' was resplendent. We thought her as beautiful as any fairy queen and the sweets placed beneath her wide skirt almost too precious to eat. The long years of war deprived us of many pleasures but that of 'our beautiful lady' taking her place each Christmas was one it didn't take away, nor will time ever do so; in the memory of childhood she still enchants.

Was the trouble over Joan's name merely a slight hiccup during a christening ceremony, or a portent of things to come?

The coming was not delayed.

Cutting of teeth is a painful process for children and Joan was no exception. A crust cut into fingers and left in the side oven of the grate to become rock hard served in place of teething rings and when this failed to soothe, the sore gums were massaged with a forefinger.

The problem really began, however, when the teeth finally erupted. Like a puppy, Joan tried them out on every thing she could hold. Cups would be gleefully handed back with bits missing from the rim, saucers likewise; the snap as chunks were bitten from drinking glasses brought giggles of delight from Joan and sighs of exasperation from Mother.

Situated next to the kitchen and empty during the time the rest of the family were at work or at school, the bathroom became a play area when the weather was too wet or too cold for outdoors. The bathroom held no pills or potions, therefore it caused no real concern when, me being at school, three-year-old Joan went one morning to play there alone.

Suspicion did not dawn until silence reigned. The babble of words that were the constant companion of play no longer issued from behind the door separating bathroom from kitchen. Mother called but received no answer. Listening for a moment she called again and then went into the bathroom.

Joan's new game was revealed.

Standing on the stool Mother used when bathing us younger ones, Joan had reached up to the window sill and the packet of razor blades Father kept there.

'Me do!' Joan lifted one last razor blade to her mouth, beamed triumphantly and said, 'Me do again eh?'

Should Mother scream or should she faint?

Glancing at the remnants of scalpel-sharp steel lying in the washbasin, then at the whole blade poised so near her daughter's mouth, Mother realised the former might well serve to have the hand holding the razor blade jerk and slash Joan's face, happily smiling, while the latter would serve no purpose at all.

Trying to keep fear from her voice and every trace of scolding from her tone, she held out the promise of a Farley's Rusk in exchange for the blade. This saw it carefully retrieved and the bathroom door securely closed . . . until the next time!

A year or so following the razor-blade incident, Mother was offered half a dozen newly hatched chicks. With rationing in force, food was limited and eggs, always presuming they were to be had, restricted to one per person per week. If they could be reared to become hens who would then lay eggs and thus supplement meals the chicks were immediately accepted.

Mother obtained a cardboard box in which was

placed a dry floor mop for the chicks to nestle under during the night, and placed the said box in the bathroom where the heat of the hot water tank would help keep the tiny creatures warm.

So far so good.

Beneath Mother's careful eye we were allowed to watch the fluffy yellow balls feed and chirp in their box. Two weeks after their first being brought into the house, Joan found the bathroom door not quite so securely closed. Watching baby chicks chase each other about was fun and with Mother gone to the gate to collect bread from the baker's cart, Joan took the opportunity to slip unseen into forbidden territory.

But chicks who had doubled in size were not so docile as when she had been allowed to stroke a gentle finger over their downy backs. These silly things kept running away.

Determination, however, brought its reward. A chick was caught and summarily released when it pecked a small finger. They had not done that before!

Deciding on the next to be lifted from the box, Joan received another sharp peck.

Joan did not like that, she did not like that at all! This wasn't the way it was supposed to go! Indignant at such antisocial behaviour and telling the chicks so, Joan caught one and of course the next peck was delivered. Big mistake! Teeth which had formerly been used in play now became weapons of vengeance.

Returned from her chat with the baker, Mother heard a squawk from the slightly open bathroom door. Dropping the loaf onto the table she rushed into the bathroom to discover Joan, a chick's neck caught between her teeth, its companions lying headless at her feet.

'They bited me!' Wide blue eyes stared unrepentantly at Mother. 'They bited me so I bited them!'

Distressing as the rest of us knew this latest act to have been for Mother, we couldn't resist stifled giggles when Phoebe's bedtime story of George the Dragon Slayer was changed to Joan the Chicken Slayer.

Piddle and plaster might have become a thing of the past but mischief was alive, happy and following close on Ann's heels.

One such episode followed her decision to become a hairdresser.

Joan, the youngest member of the family, was three years old. A slightly built child with waist-length blond hair, wide blue eyes and a ready smile, she was pretty as a picture.

But it was a picture Ann, at nine years of age, decided would be improved upon.

Told they were going to play a game, Joan happily joined her big sister beneath the kitchen table.

'You have to sit still or you can't play!' The ultimatum was obeyed, Joan being delighted to be included in any game played by 'the big ones'. Safely ensconced beyond the sight of Mother, Ann produced the scissors craftily hidden beneath her cardigan. Soon they emerged from the 'salon'; Joan's long tresses lay where they had fallen while she, smiling and innocent, bore a close resemblance to a cabbage patch doll. Mother's cries on seeing the results of Ann's handiwork and the dire threats they carried put an end to yet one more proposed career in beauty culture.

The ability to find mischief was not confined to the home, school also was fertile ground. First thing every morning and then each afternoon came handkerchief and hand inspection. Back and front, hands were scrutinised by the class teacher, any hint of dirt and you were sent into the corridor to wash and wash again with soap and cold water. Grubby fingers, though loudly decried before the rest of the class, did not carry the awesome penalty which grime beneath the fingernails called for. Each guilty finger examined in turn, supported on the end of a wooden ruler as though infected with bubonic plague, the culprit was finally ordered to report to the headmistress.

Now, a mile and a half journey to school without walking the narrow ledge of the railway bridge which stood some forty feet above the busy Monway Line carrying molten waste from that steel works, or running your hand along metal railings, or simply touching against a dusty frame as you gazed longingly into the window of Kay's shop at sweets you had no money to buy was difficult for any kid; for Ann it was impossible. How, then, to avoid an unpleasant situation?

Two methods were devised. One, spit on the hem of a petticoat and use this as a flannel. Two, pick a quarrel with another girl and in the ensuing skirmish take her handkerchief to scrub away telltale marks. Either way was, for Ann, preferable to the inevitable result of presenting dirty hands or the ultimate transgression of being without a handkerchief. Who says crime does not pay? For Ann it seemed to have paid well enough for wasn't it she who won the class prize of an Oxo painting book, presented for having the best-kept hands?

Those early desires for a career in the world of fashion and beauty, or for teacher approval, proved a stepping stone for mischief. Soon, Ann had an entire pathway! A broken arm, a thigh badly cut on barbed wire, jumping the brook only to fall in then arrive home looking like a drowned rat, were the traditional hallmarks of growing up in the Black Country: they raised neither eyebrow nor temper. But the following example of behaviour raised the headmistress's ire and Mother's fury.

Part of the war effort was the urging of people to

put money into government saving bonds. It goes without saying the Astbury girls were never in the line-up to pay a weekly contribution into the school savings bank. Although Ann was by no means the only girl in her class of whom this was true, it rankled, for there would be a prize for whoever saved the most money in the year.

Hazel Turner's older sister had saved for months in order to provide herself with a white wedding. Withdrawing every penny of this from the Post Office she gave it to Hazel, thus boosting her school savings so she became the winner of a 'silver' shield. So incensed by what she saw as unfair competition, Ann allowed jealousy to win the day. Hazel Turner took home not only the shield but also a pummelling from Ann.

This could not go unremarked. Called next day to the headmistress's room Ann took further exception to Miss Harris's justifiable anger. Upon being asked to account for her behaviour Ann's reply was silence. The ensuing reprimand adding insult to injury Ann lost the plot. Out came the words 'Oh S . . .!'

A swear word! The most heinous of sins in a church school. Shock or outrage had Miss Harris declare, 'That sort of language is more suited to Holyhead Road school, perhaps you should attend there in future.'

Antipathy towards Holyhead Road school was something that those pupils of St James' school who, like us, lived in Dangerfield Lane or its near environs did not understand, yet with being continually instructed 'not to have anything to do with those Holyhead Road children' we were under no illusions as to its existence or the snobbery behind it. A council school, it did not have the ethos of a long-established church school. But the children you were ordered to ignore were the very ones you lived next to, the ones you played with in the street.

But going against a teacher's instruction invited repercussions, especially when that instruction was given by the headmistress. So, taking this command literally, Ann duly arrived at Holyhead Road the following day.

Miss Harris's discomfort upon receiving a telephone call from the headteacher saying a certain Ann Astbury was in his school – and why – could only be guessed. Mother's reaction, however, was tangible; once more Ann was threatened with every punishment imaginable. Fortunately for her, as with any of us guilty of misbehaviour, Mother's anger rarely found expression in a slap. It always gave way to, 'I'll tell your father the minute he comes in!'

But Father wouldn't be in for hours. The employment he had found with the recently opened Newman's Tube Works meant he would not come home before seven. This was where breath eased in the lungs of the culprit, for Father always came up with a feasible excuse followed by a carefully hidden wink.

Hidden did I say? Not from Mother. She didn't miss a trick. Passing the buck to Father was her way of saving herself the heartache of punishing any of the daughters both she and George adored.

7

Chitterlings and Chips

Feeding a growing family with the only regular source of income being 'labour money' (dole) must have been a nightmare for Mother. Father, it has to be said, would take on any work offered but in the economic slump of the late twenties and early thirties the numbers of men flocking to the promise of a day's employment were like flies around a jam pot.

It is obvious, then, that no table Mother or Father knew boasted meals fit for a king. But somehow or other they managed, Father always sharing his plate with us kids while Mother, saying she had eaten already, many times went without. This state of affairs was not restricted to one family; there were many others with the same dilemma. Yet somehow food of a sort was found. We in this fast food era might not find some of yesterday's fare to our modern taste but eighty-plus years ago it filled many a hungry belly.

Chitterlings were one such dish. The small intestines of pig, they were washed in salted water and when thoroughly cleaned were plaited and looped. This done, they were usually cooked slowly in a tepid oven and served hot with onion and vegetables which were often got from a neighbour's allotment, swapped in exchange for ''alf a yard o' chitterlin''.

There were so many meals that could be got from a pig. Take faggots. This particular dish, though no delicacy, was a favourite. Mouths would drool at the aroma drifting from the kitchen on a cold winter evening and truth be told, mine drools now at the memory. Made from fry (heart, liver and lights) chopped with onions, a slice of stale bread and seasoned with salt, pepper, sage and bay leaf, the mixture was rolled into portions the size of a snooker ball then wrapped in kell, the delicate lacy lining of the stomach. Cooked slowly then served with 'blue' peas (known more recently as mushy peas), this was a feast none of us kids would swap for the king's dinner.

The pig supplied many meals, but few of them in the form of a roast. Dangerfield Lane of the early thirties hardly knew a leg of roast pork but good use was made of feet, tails, for broth, kidney for suet puddings, heart boiled and sliced, even bones became boney pie, and of course there was always lard. Rendered from cooking ribs, seasoned with salt and pepper and spread on a 'noggin' of bread it provided sandwiches which served for morning break in factory, or in my own case a toasted slice before leaving for school.

But the best bit of all was the 'crackling', the skin of the animal. Eyes would light up at the sight of a plate of this. Broken carefully into pieces of as near equal size as Mother could make them, they were mouth-watering – a gift from the gods indeed. A gift still enjoyed today and over a far wider area than the Black Country, for what was once a part of the pork joint is now almost always stripped away at the abattoir and sold to food-processing plants. These in turn cook and market the resulting crackling in small packets seen in many supermarkets, clubs and pubs. If you have never tasted crackling then give it a go, I think you will agree with me that it is a pleasant taste of yesterday.

These dishes are by no means all the pig provided; the list only ended when the entire carcass was finished. Like Father always said, 'The only part of a pig you can't eat is its grunt.' But one especial delicacy was the brain. How my father enjoyed this meal! Again they had to be thoroughly cleaned before being wrapped in a clean white (always white) cloth and boiled for fifteen minutes. Served with chopped hard-boiled egg and slices of bread and butter they were delicious.

The Lane and its immediate surroundings was what I think of, looking back, as a self-sufficient community. Women, each striving to feed a family, would often specialise in one field or another. Living at number fifty-three, the daughter of the family would collect the Monday morning bundle from any family (and there were many) who needed the loan of money from the pawn shop in Church Street, Darlaston. She would then redeem the items for those same families on Friday evenings when the weekly pay was brought home. This service paid sixpence, a charge of threepence a journey. At number forty-nine, Harry could make almost anything from scrap metal.

An only child, as far as I know, Harry was the son of Harold and Ada Timmins. Quiet, likeable, Harry was quite a mechanic. A wooden box fixed to a metal bed mounted on wheels provided a trolley for use in fetching coal from Bache's wharf some half a mile away; fix a seat to a similar construction and it became a 'racing motor' much beloved by lads in the street. A flat piece of metal, the edges hammered over to prevent young hands from being scratched, one end drilled so rope or string could be attached, made a sledge with which to slide down the 'grassy knobs' – waste heaps left from coal mining and now covered with grass – a source of continual pleasure.

Harry could be relied upon to straighten the bent prongs of a garden fork, to replace a jagged spade plate with one he made himself, to mend broken toys.

or make new parts for ones lost. Wednesbury and Darlaston had a multiplicity of steel works, the night watchmen of these voicing no objection to Harry's 'tekin' a little bit'.

Neighbours and their children appreciated Harry's skills, but none more so than myself when his tinkering resulted in a bicycle that he gave to me. Reconstructed from bits gathered from heaven knows where, it was my pride and joy. I often think of Harry Timmins and hope his life has been as happy as he helped make that of the Dangerfield Lane kids.

Nearer the Darlaston end of the Lane lived a family named Weaver. Mrs Weaver made pikelets, brought to your door by her son, who carried them in a large wicker laundry basket covered over with a checked cloth. The pikelets she made were virtually the same as those produced commercially today and marketed as crumpets, though here in the heart of the Black Country we still buy them under the old name. Toasted on a fork held before an open fire, then spread thickly with butter so it soaked well into the holes with which the dough was pitted in the cooking, Mrs Weaver's pikelets were delicious; they made Sunday teatime a feast.

This family boasted its own pig. They would collect any waste vegetable matter, fruit core, peelings and stale bread (supposing any ever got to that stage) and in exchange you got a cut from the pig butchered for Christmas.

Towards the middle of the Lane was Court's Farm. What a delight for kids surrounded by factories belching smoke to watch a herd of cows being driven across the road to the milking sheds. A penny would buy a jug of warm milk or a pot of freshly made butter; though when there was no penny, as was often the case, the same could be exchanged for some commodity, maybe a faggot or two or a plate of boney pie.

'Granny' Melia lived in St John's Alley. Her speciality was faggots and peas. Buried beneath a mountain of laundry draped over the 'bow', a waist-high fireguard which enclosed the front of the black lead grate, Mother was sometimes too busy to cook. This meant the first home from school was handed a jug and a threepenny piece, then sent off to collect a jug of faggots.

Close by the farm lived Ben, a young man rather cruelly nicknamed Benny Duckegg. I never did know why. It was said he was a bookies' runner – bookmaking was illegal in those days – so perhaps always being on the watch for the 'bobbies' caused Ben to appear shifty. Whatever the reason, youngsters took to their heels at the call, 'Hey up, Benny's coming!'

Everybody paid into the 'Death and Divi'. No matter how or from where it came, folk had to afford that penny a week. Payment from the D&D club together with the few coppers neighbours contributed to the usual street collection, was often the only way a funeral could be paid for. Each Saturday morning, a sprightly Granny Smith would call at the house to collect the weekly contribution, half an hour's chat keeping Mother abreast of any new developments, social or otherwise, taking place in the vicinity of the Lane. This was enjoyable if not strictly necessary: the grapevine was liberally tended by others calling to ask did Mother 'want anything bringing from up the town'.

Seventy years ago neighbours were not simply anonymous figures seen only entering or leaving their houses, nor were those homes the closely secured premises we know today. Doors were left unlocked and in summer regularly open. A milk bottle left an hour longer than usual on a doorstep would herald an enquiring visit, the call from the door asking, 'Is everythin' all right?' Illness in the home, especially should the sick person be a child, brought a bevy of offers of help; money was always in short supply but friendly assistance never was.

Granny and Aunt were titles of respect children were taught to adopt when referring to or addressing neighbours who were not blood relatives. Every kid had a wealth of these, but one was a confirmed favourite.

Chitterlings and Chips

Granny Bird lived in Margaret Road. Before rationing restricted the supply of sugar, sweets of almost every kind could be had from Granny Bird. A long trestle table ran the length of her living room and my nose reached just to the edge of it.

'What'n yoh be wantin', mah babby?' Shawl draped over her shoulders, grey hair scraped to the back of her head, she would smile over her Aladdin's Cave of home-made toffee, boiled sweets, lollipops and bullseyes, her patience never flagging while you stood clutching a farthing, your eyes as wide as the many coloured gob-stoppers.

Today we are bombarded with advertisements for every kind of confection, the media of television and press show foods our parents could not even dream of, but not one of these provides the pleasure of the treasured memories of childhood. The aroma of 'grorty pudding', a thick stew of groats, onion and the trimmings of beef, or of a pan of 'grey' peas embellished with bacon bits, can still make my mouth water.

But of all the dishes I have mentioned and the many more I have not, the best had to be Mother's contribution to the exchange and mart. She cooked fish and roe. A drop of home-made beer added to a mixture of flour, water and a touch of colouring which I can only guess was cochineal, made batter so deliciously crisp it had your taste buds singing.

Chips were also given a light toss in remnants of batter clinging to the bowl so they crunched between the teeth. So popular were Mother's fish and chips that she cooked almost every night, supplying neighbours waiting with plates at the kitchen door. A piece of fish and a few chips welcomed many a husband home in the evening.

Then there were the children. If the question, 'Is yoh'r mother mekin' chips?' was met with an affirmative, then there would be half a dozen standing armed with a piece of newspaper and sniffing longingly at the salt-and-vinegar-scented air drifting from the kitchen. Mother could never refuse. Folding their piece of paper into the shape of an ice-cream cornet, she would fill it with chips. The children never brought a copper nor any article of food as payment, yet not one went away empty handed.

But it was not only fish and chips Mother's kitchen was noted for; it also provided many a jug of home-brewed ale, stout, ginger beer and lemonade much relished by neighbours of all ages.

The barter system flourished throughout the Lane, continuing through the years of economic depression and the earlier ones of the war, but with the bite of food rationing it gradually petered out. Two ounces of margarine, one ounce of butter, a slice of bacon or a sausage if you were lucky, hardly left anything to barter with. Still somehow Mother managed, sometimes with a rabbit or a fish caught by a friend of Father and given to 'mek a meal for yoh'r babbies'.

Of course the Black Market soon made its appearance and thanks to those same friends our rations were sometimes supplemented with a tin of corned beef, dried egg or the odd packet of Woodbine cigarettes for Father, all welcome gifts. We never questioned the method of supply or which lorry they had 'fallen from the back of'. The years of hardship, of making do with fresh air, had taught a bitter lesson: you took what providence allowed.

Mother, with five children and a husband to feed, would accept with gratitude and not a few tears. And always you would hear her quietly whispered, 'God's good, if He don't come then He sends.'

8

Saga of a Chicken

In the early thirties, employment in Wednesbury had become more difficult to find than elves at the bottom of a garden. Day after day Father tramped in search of a job, any job that would feed his family; but day upon day saw factory gates closed, notices hung on them reading 'no hands required'.

Fruitless as the effort was it still had to be tried, that was until shoes which had long lost their soles finally gave up the ghost; the uppers broke completely apart. This disaster was threefold. Without shoes, how could he search for work? Without shoes, how could he collect the family benefit? Without presenting himself at the relevant office that money would not be paid, not even the one shilling allowance for each child. Women were not allowed to collect in place of a husband, so it was no use Mother attempting to do so.

No food in the house, no money in Mother's purse, the situation was hopeless.

Then Father remembered the box kept beneath the cold slab in the pantry. Houses in Dangerfield Lane often saw bathrooms and pantries being used for purposes in addition to those originally intended. Number 51 was no exception. The box stored in this one held odd bits and pieces we used in dressing-up games and among this assortment was a pair of shoes donated by Mother's sister Phoebe.

In times of desperation pride has no place.

Taking out the shoes, Father hammered off the heels. Forcing his size seven feet into size five black suede court-style shoes, he made the journey to Knowles Street returning with bruised and bleeding toes. Yet neither injury to pride nor to feet had prevented his calling at the Shambles to buy that treat we kids drooled over – the pound of sausages.

Lack of money affected birthdays and Christmas. Knowing Mother would have provided something for the socks hung from the fireplace, I must admit in all honesty I have few early memories of anything other than an orange, a few nuts and a bright shining new penny, though I do recall one year being given a doll in a pram. Feeling like a princess, I wheeled this wonderful gift along the street. A few doors along Leach's son Billy barred my way. Usually friendly, Billy now wore an expression that boded trouble.

He demanded to be told where the shining dark blue pram had come from and he snorted at the answer.

'Ain't no Father Christmas!' He raised an angry

fist. 'Ain't no Father Christmas!' The fist came down straight through the hood of my beautiful doll's pram.

Though by no means brand new, probably got for a few coppers or even in payment for some job or other done by Father then secretly cleaned by Mother and hidden away until 'Father Christmas could deliver it', my pram was to me nothing short of magnificent. To see its hood torn and Billy laugh reduced me to tears.

'I can mend it,' Mother comforted. 'Of course Father Christmas won't stop coming. No, he will not think you broke it.'

It took some time before my tears dried, but not as long as it took Billy's, or for the bottom his mother walloped to stop stinging. Kids would always be kids and a moment of jealousy was not a good enough reason for friction between neighbours – their world held troubles enough. Wisely, they decided to count the incident forgotten. I wonder, did Billy ever forget?

There were other gifts: for example, a needlework box and a prophetic blackboard and easel, but these came in later years when Hilda and Phoebe were at work, thus contributing to the housekeeping.

I think Betty must have been a birthday present. A straw-filled body, painted plaster moon face and a hole in one arm, she had obviously seen owners before me but I treasured her none the less.

It was the hole in the arm that probably aroused my

desire for nursing. Dye had often to prove the solution for 'new' curtains and with the onset of war and clothing coupons it had to be used for clothing, too; an old dress or faded coat revived to live another few years thanks to a bottle of dye.

These slim glass phials, bought from the chemist and containing powdered dye, inspired a new game of nurse. A collection of these glass tubes with tiny cork stoppers, each of which held a small amount of coloured water Mother saved when rinsing a freshly dyed article, became my pharmacy. Lined along the window sill, the variety of colours added interest to Betty's 'medicines', which were administered a few precious drops at a time. The fact they never entered those closed lips, that they dripped down that plaster chin, made no difference.

Neither did the 'ointments' applied to the arm. Concocted from baking powder, flour, starch or indeed anything which would mix with a little melted lard or camphorated oil to produce a gooey cream, this was applied to the 'injury', then bandaged over with strips of rag.

Finally, I came to acknowledge that creams and medicines were having no effect, no doubt helped by Mother's insistence that the process ended before I too came to need nursing against some awful infection! So the offending goo was washed away and the arm completely dried out. Then Betty underwent surgery. A needle, a length of black cotton and Doctor Margaret stitched the hole; stitches large enough to hold the Titanic together detracted not a jot from my pride at accomplishing the satisfaction of the successful 'operation'.

Having no brothers to fight our battles meant having to learn to stick up for ourselves. That was a lesson we each learned with alacrity.

From earliest childhood, the problems of one became the problems of her sisters and each helped in the solving, no less when the solving meant fighting. If one of us was hit by another youngster, that meant all-out war. Hilda, the eldest and with a sense of responsibility towards her younger sisters, would wade in, closely followed by the others all with fists flying, none giving up until the battle was won. No one, whether male or female, was allowed to 'have a go' at either sister and get off scot free. Avenging angels? There were times Mother's daughters could have given even them a lesson!

That one maxim, 'you stick together', followed all through our years of growing. A bond was forged between five sisters, a bond made of the love of a mother and father. It bound us close and has never once failed; it holds as firmly today as it ever did: one hint of trouble, one whisper of unhappiness and from each end of the country we come sticking together to sort out the problem. Sisters, as Mother and Father would have wanted.

But for all the scrapes and battles I got into, and there were many, I never fought with Peter.

The son of Paddy and Gladys Noon, Peter lived at Number 47. He had light brown hair and brown eyes, his slightly stocky build was a match for my own, and we grew to teen years like brother and sister, he as much at home in our house as in his own. I suppose we had our disagreements – knowing my own bossy ways as a youngster it would be wrong to claim we absolutely did not – yet I cannot remember our ever having a dispute. If we did, it certainly did not carry over any length of time, Peter being of a quiet, less fiery nature than myself.

Looking back, it seems we spent a great deal of time in each other's company; playing cowboys and Indians – no prize for guessing who played the Indian – hide and seek, along with other kids of the lane all utilising neighbours' gardens for places to hide; marbles, five jacks, any and every street game we played together.

Then there were the group jaunts. At eleven or twelve we felt ourselves very grown up and Sunday expeditions to Baggeridge Wood, Sutton Coldfield or Walsall Arboretum became a regular weekend activity, Hilda and Phoebe stumping up the pennies I needed for bus fares out of the allowance they were given back from the wages they earned. There was no such thing as paying board in those days, pay packets were handed over, unopened, in their entirety.

Ours was a close, happy friendship which began after Peter suffered an accident.

While still at the toddling stage, Peter reached up to the pan of water boiling on his mother's stove. Her cries brought my own mother rushing to the house. There she stripped the clothes from the screaming boy, proceeded to smother the whole of his body with Robin's Starch, then wrapped him in a clean sheet.

Why Robin's Starch? Mothers of Dangerfield Lane children possessed no such niceties as baby powder. Mother's first aid would today be frowned upon, but for Peter it worked.

One of the pastimes Peter and I shared was the keeping of pigeons. In those days girls never wore trousers (except those of the Land Army uniform) but I was different. Racing home from school, I was straight into a pair from a jumble sale and out into our back garden, where an old china cabinet housed several birds given to my father.

Father's interests being dominoes and cards, he had no leaning towards joining the ranks of pigeon fanciers. Yet, loath to refuse the gift he brought them home where he promptly presented them to me, and consequently to Peter. Rolling and tumbling in flight these birds were a source of pride and pleasure to

Mom and Dad on their wedding day 28 June 1925

Joan

Phoebe

Hilda

Me

Ann

Annie's Wenches

Pitt Square, 1933

St Bartholomew's, Wednesbury

No. 110 Leabrook Road

Rear of Portway Road, Wednesbury

Coal Picking

Coal Jagger, Wednesbury

Leabrook Furnaces and Canal

Women Colliery Surface Workers

Market Place, Wednesbury

51 Dangerfield Road

St James' School

St James' Church

Peter and myself – we would have them peck corn from our ears and hair while imitating their call. Then one night they were stolen. This was no isolated case, there had been quite a spate of thefts from the lofts of men whose brand of sport was pigeon racing, but when it happened to us I was devastated.

Situated at the part of Wednesbury known locally as the White Horse, a hotel of that name being something of a landmark, the police station was a couple of miles from Dangerfield Lane but Peter and I trudged our way there in the dark.

We reported the theft to a policeman, giving a description of each bird's colouring. He smiled when I added 'the red hen is in lay'. I had no idea what that meant but it sounded important and fortunately the constable conscientiously writing down all we said did not ask me to explain.

We never did recover our pigeons. They no doubt were sold to the 'cage', a shop in Darlaston's Pinfold Street which sold several sort of animals and birds. For Peter and me the pigeon-keeping days had come to an unexpected halt, but our friendship continued until a heart attack ended his life in his mid-thirties. No, ended is too final a word. The friendship that existed between us can never be forgotten. I have treasured it all of my life and will continue to do so.

So the pigeons were gone, but not so the china cabinet. That witnessed a new lease of life when

Mother once again embarked upon the tricky business of raising poultry.

These would provide good meals when the chicks were fully grown. But chickens have to be killed before they can be cooked.

'You'll 'ave to do it!'

Father blinked at the no-nonsense order, his face blanching white as the long-bladed kitchen knife was held out to him.

Now Father could never hurt a fly and the thought of cutting the throat of a chicken turned his stomach. But unpleasant as this prospect was, the anger of his wife should he refuse was more so.

Armed with the knife he went down to the china cabinet. He would grab a bird and, with eyes closed, would do the fatal deed. But as he opened the door, six startled hens made for freedom. Pandemonium followed. Clucking loudly, wings flapping, Father chasing, they raced around the garden, always managing to evade the hand that reached for them.

Ten minutes later he was no nearer fulfilling his mission. There was only one thing for it.

Knocking at next door he handed the knife to Fred. The son of Dickie and Nanny Harris, Fred always helped when asked and Father was asking now. But Father was still not off the hook.

'You hold it.' Fred at last had caught one of the squawking fowl. 'You hold it an' I'll kill it.'

But how did you hold a mass of heaving feathers? Eventually the matter was solved. The chicken's body held fast between his knees, Father waited with gritted teeth, one hand grasping its head and pulling until the neck stretched.

Then the knife sliced down. Revulsion at the feel of the jerking body made Father release the pressure of his knees. The headless body ran in several circles before finally becoming still.

Father never assisted at the slaughter of another chicken.

9

A Visit to the Library

Shortage of money ever the wraith that stalked many folk of the Black Country, children sent to perform any errand which involved the use of cash were given the grave command to 'tek care o' that money!' This same caution was one day given Hilda.

After school she was told to collect groceries from Dudley Street, the shop Mother had used when living in Pitt's Square; she was then to bring them straight home to Dangerfield Lane.

The precious ten-shilling note was tucked between the pages of a library book which was to be returned after school that same afternoon, so Hilda had no fears for its safety.

School dismissed, Hilda went first to the library. Engrossed in the fascinating world of books, the delicious task of choosing one for herself meant time became lost in this world of delights and no thought of groceries encroached upon that pleasure. She completely forgot the banknote placed between the pages of her book until she had almost reached home.

A thunderbolt could not have worried her more. The value of money was a lesson she had learned early and that ten-shilling note would be all the money Mother had.

Running back along the Bilston Road, across the High Bullen and on to the library Hilda prayed constantly the money would be waiting safely.

She explained matters to the librarian who found the book. She took it from the shelf and handed it to Hilda. Hands trembling, heart pounding, she rifled the pages as the librarian watched. The pages were rifled again.

Was she sure this was the book she had returned? Lips caught between her teeth, tears of desperation glinting in her eyes, Hilda could only nod.

Taking the book from her, holding it by the covers, the librarian shook it. The pages flapped. Hilda watched. Nothing fluttered to the ground. The ten-shilling note was gone!

You couldn't blame Mother for her reaction. There was no charity that would feed her kids, no philanthropic society to step in replacing what was lost. Stress won a momentary battle. The kitchen knife she had been using while listening to the whimpered account of the lost note still in her hand, her face rapidly lost its colour.

Worry which had grown with every step of the way back from the library now turned to fear in Hilda.

Mother was kind and gentle – until something aroused her temper. Not waiting to find out if losing that money would be one of those somethings, Hilda took to her heels running to grandmother's new council house in Margaret Road.

Mother set off in hot pursuit to be met by Mary Ann, a frightened granddaughter protected behind wide black skirts.

Half crying, half shouting, Mother declared her intention of 'knockin' some sense into 'er!'

Mary Ann's reply was calm as her daughter's was agitated.

'Oh ar,' she said, 'but yoh'r goin' to 'ave to knock every bit out of me first. This babby d'aint lose that money on purpose and 'er be not to blame; the fault be your own. You wants groceries then fetch 'em yourself, don't leave a wench to do it for ya!'

I don't know how we got food enough for that week. No doubt Grandmother and neighbours shared with us the little they themselves had.

Mother's anger was washed away by Mary Ann's common sense and the threatened hiding was forgotten, but for Hilda the worry her carelessness had caused was not. This was to be proved in a relatively short time.

The shop in Dudley Street was a good mile and a half from the house in Dangerfield Lane, a journey Mother, with her crippled leg, found increasingly difficult. Therefore, despite Mary Ann's sharp words, Hilda was once more relied upon to bring home the required groceries. This time there would be no library visit, nothing to claim her concentration. But concentration was not all that was needed.

After she'd done the shopping and was passing the closely packed houses of Portway Road, Hilda was accosted by a boy. Taller and heavier than his victim he saw the basket as an easy prize demanding it be handed over.

Another week's groceries lost! Grandmother might not save her from Mother's anger a second time! That prospect was more frightening than any lad.

Making his demand a second time he was surprised when it was refused, a surprise intensified by the kick with which his grab for the basket was met. But he wasn't to forgo all of that prize. Grabbing the topmost package, he darted into an entry adjoining two houses.

The soap! She dared not go home without it.

This thought uppermost, Hilda set the basket on the footpath and ran after the jeering thief, up the entry, across a shared yard and into the house. Watched by his parents, brothers and sisters she chased him around the table until he was caught by the scruff of the neck, his father demanding to know the cause of the rumpus.

The soap was handed back and by some miracle

the basket of groceries stood untouched where she had left it.

Don't let yourself be bullied. Another valuable lesson had been learned.

IO

Chief Sitting Bull

The years of childhood for the Astbury girls held none of the expensive toys, games and technological equipment that the modern youngster declares essential. Street games with no more than a ball or marbles were all that was available, but they were by no means the only source of entertainment, or at least not in our house. One game that gave us a great deal of enjoyment was cowboys and Indians, though Mother was always glad when the entertainment was over and peace declared between the two.

Feathers and war whoops added to the excitement, but a little more realism came when we found a bottle of nail varnish. This was something new in the house so when Ann brought it in, having picked it up from the street on her way home from school, we were all eager to try it.

Whose could it have been? Holyhead Road was a busy link between many towns, anyone travelling it could be the owner of that nail polish so how did we find that owner? Should we ask around? Take the bottle to the police? Mother finally settled the matter. Whoever had once owned that nail varnish might have thrown it out deliberately, and anyway the whole affair was too insignificant to trouble the police with. And no, we definitely could not paint our nails!

It was an evening or two after making the find that Father agreed to a game of cowboys and Indians. Hilda and Phoebe plumped for being cowboys, Ann and I were to be Indian braves while Joan, too small to join in the tribal dance and dash around the table and through the kitchen, was pacified by having a feather stuck in a band around her head and being sat safely on Mother's knee.

Guns were represented by an extended forefinger and a shouted 'bang,' bows by one arm extended while the other was drawn back, hand against the shoulder, a pronounced 'whoosh' indicating the release of an arrow.

The game would then follow its usual course: 'pow-wow', with Father's peace pipe – a cigarette – and the cowboys nodding then raising their right hands and saying solemnly 'How!' But as in the best stories negotiations would fail and the inevitable clash ensue.

This one evening things did not follow the usual course. Big Chief Sitting Bull (Father) spotted the bottle on the shelf above the fireplace.

War paint!

Within moments his forehead and cheeks were traced with broad scarlet lines. The artistic interpretation of a war chief was excellent and we all enjoyed the skirmish which eventually ended amicably, as always.

Ten minutes later we discovered the reason for Mother's absolute refusal to let us paint our fingernails. Father's face, though painfully red from scrubbing, had not relinquished one iota of nail varnish and we had no such thing as nail varnish remover.

Not even a striped face was allowed to keep him from work, though it became several shades redder when workmates greeted him with cries of 'How', then chanted 'ha-ha-ooh-oa' as they performed a war dance around the stove.

It was not only games of cowboys and Indians Father was ready to join in, he was also quite adept at dancing. A soft shoe shuffle with flat cap and bamboo bean stick in place of top hat and cane was one speciality. Another was that favourite of the twenties, the black bottom. He would demonstrate this dance while humming his own accompaniment. But it was what followed that afforded the greater amusement. Mother would fasten a strip of cloth around our brows adorning them with fragments of peacock feather she had kept in a cupboard for years, then all five of us formed a chorus line and Father would proceed to teach us the steps. Despite all efforts I never did master the black bottom.

The same can be said of another dance class.

Called the 'Clapperettes', this was a group of tap dance enthusiasts drawn together by Joe Johnson, lessons being given in his home at Wood's Bank near to Catherine's Cross. Phoebe, Ann and friends all joined the group, saving pennies earned from all and every errand to buy steel taps which Father nailed to the heels and tips of the soles of their shoes.

As I listened to them tell Mother of the routines they were being taught, and heard the excitement in their voices as they spoke of the dance teacher's aspirations for a theatre show, I caught the bug. I too wanted to be a 'Clapperette'.

Phoebe was especially reluctant to agree to take me along. Feeling grown up at fourteen she didn't want an eight year old hanging onto her coat tails while she chatted up the boys outside of Peoli's ice-cream parlour! So although the three of us left the house together, Ann was passed the responsibility of looking after me.

I was welcomed by Joe's mother. Always present at rehearsals, she encouraged my efforts. Joe, however, was sceptical; he didn't need to be an expert to see I possessed the proverbial two left feet which, regardless of the direction the rest of the troupe took, always insisted on turning the wrong way. To this day, I still have trouble telling left from right . . .

For the first few practice evenings, Joe was encouraging, but when my dumpy legs continued to refuse to lift me into jump turns and my feet didn't quite get the hang of the heel-toe-tap routine he suggested it might be better for me to take a singing spot in the proposed musical production.

'Daddy wouldn't Buy me a Bow-Wow.'

For weeks I sang that same song, obediently following Joe's suggestions for movement about the stage, the use of varied nuances of expression until eventually I couldn't have wanted a 'bow-wow' less!

The performing bug had died!

Life without television, computer games, and pop videos – youngsters today might find that inconceivable, yet that was exactly how it was. True, there were theatres, music halls and cinemas, but none of these offered free admission and unless a thing were free of charge then it was closed to the Astbury family. The children of Annie and George were obliged, as were all the kids of Dangerfield Lane, to make their own entertainment.

The streets were our playground, providing a venue for ball games until the owner of the ball objected to something or other and withdrew indoors, the ball disappearing alongside. Then it would be Tin

Can Lurky. A house brick supported a tin can on which was balanced a stick. Players took turns to throw pebbles at the can. With every lucky strike they scattered, the game then being to recapture the players in order to start all over again.

Tip Cat was a competitive game. A stick and a small piece of wood was all a player required. The starting point would be marked by a stone or line of pebbles. One by one you placed your 'cat' – the small wedge of wood – level with the start line then struck it with the stick, tipping the 'cat' into the air. As it rose you then whacked it as hard as you could. The contestant whose 'cat' travelled furthest was of course the winner.

To play 'Off Horses' needed no equipment, which made it a favourite among us kids. The walls that edged the gardens of houses in the Lane were topped with concrete blocks in a crenellated design. The spaces between accommodated the bottoms of spectators to any street game. Looking back on some of those games now, I wonder how we escaped injury. 'Off Horses' was one such. Bent over from the waist, head positioned between outstretched arms, the 'horse' would hold both hands to the wall. The riders would stand in line and call 'on horse'; then vault onto the bent-over back, aiming to get as far onto the shoulders as possible. This gave ample room for the next rider and the next until, legs buckling the 'horse' would shout 'off horse' and at least four bodies would tumble laughing onto the pavement. How many bad backs have their origins in that game?

That was risky enough, but think on this one.

Winter meant dark evenings, which ended the matches played with marbles or the games of 'Five Jacks' in which five pebbles (if you were very lucky you had metal jacks) were tossed into the air, the aim being to catch as many as you could on the back of your hand. This achieved, you immediately tossed them to catch them in the palm. Any jacks dropped as a result were counted as lost and set aside, the game finishing when one or other player had lost all jacks. We never went indoors until we absolutely had to, and seeing as none of us had so much as a penny to share between us the pleasures of the picture house were out of the question. That was where the Fire Can came in.

First you found your tin can. That accomplished, it was – in the case of myself and my sisters – handed to Father, who pierced the sides and bottom several times, hammering the metal through with a stout nail. Then he fastened a wire through holes close to the rim of the can, providing it with a handle. This cylindrical colander was then filled with burning coals taken from the living-room fire. These miniature braziers were our delight. We fed them throughout the evening with tiny pieces of coal, scavenged either from the pit heaps donated to the landscape by the worked-out Lodge Holes colliery, or someone's coal-house. Whirled around the head in a figure of eight they roared and flared, gleaming red, gold and blue, studding the darkness like a brilliant display of fireworks while we whooped and shouted our sheer exhilaration.

Not every game we played carried such an element of danger. For the boys, an old partly deflated ball and a couple of bricks to mark a goal area provided a game of football, brought to a halt whenever a horse-drawn cart needed to pass, or an irate householder chased them from the vicinity of a garden. Cricket, too, was popular and often fathers would join in.

Toys were practically nonexistent in those early years, money being too scarce a commodity to use on non-essentials so we learned to do without. Games such as 'Farmer in his den', 'I wrote a letter to my wife' or 'A tisket a tasket' were most usual among girls. That's when we weren't skipping.

A length of clothes line constituted the rope and the two girls first to call 'First and fourteen' became the turners. Why 'First and fourteen'? I don't know why the fourteen, but it was thought that being first to turn the rope meant your turn to skip would last that much longer . . . how we worked that out still eludes me!

Our skipping was often accompanied by rhymes, sung or chanted in unison with the turning of the rope, which again had to be halted in the event of passing traffic.

> Cherries on a plate, cherries on a plate,
> One, two, three, four cherries on a plate.

The number of cherries would increase until someone's foot caught the rope and they would be out.

One skipping rhyme, accompanied by the relevant actions, was taught us by Mother who, thanks to a considerate headmistress and her own strength of will, had eventually come to play herself, despite her disability. It went like this:

> I am a girl guide dressed in blue
> These are the things I ought to do.
> Stand at ease,
> Bend your knees,
> Salute to the King,
> Bow to the Queen,
> And turn your back on the Kaiser.

With the outbreak of the Second World War this last line was changed to the patriotic 'Turn your back on the Führer'.

The war, of course, changed many things. Fire cans could no longer be delighted in lest overhead enemy planes spot the light dancing from them. Whistles once used in games of hide and seek were banned, now to be used solely by air raid wardens. Games were in the main restricted to our own back yard and one summer saw the production of a pantomime.

It being my idea, and the theatre being the back garden of our house, yours truly being scriptwriter, director, producer, stage manager, costumier and general jack of all trades, I claimed the part of Principal Boy, other roles being allocated to those kids wanting to take part.

Every afternoon after school, and each evening until dark, we rehearsed: we were going to have the best performance of Aladdin ever staged. Chicken feathers tied with oddments of ribbon became Abanazer's hat. Widow Twanky's costume was a frock lent by one neighbour and an apron from another, while a shopping basket served for her laundry basket. Aladdin was the proposed production but somehow Cinderella and her Ugly Sisters, Snow White and the Dwarves, Red Riding Hood and Jack – though minus his Beanstalk – all managed to make an appearance.

Whatever could be spared, and more often what could be 'borrowed' without it being missed, was brought into use, bedecking us in the most unlikely costumes. Paper hats and crowns glued together with flour and water completed the outfits that made each kid a star.

But the lamp! Aladdin couldn't be Aladdin without the magic lamp. But no lamp was to be begged, borrowed or stolen.

The problem was solved one Sunday afternoon.

Going anywhere near the council rubbish tip was strictly off limits, but how was Mother to know the diversion we took on the way home from Sunday School? Anyway, you had to be caught to be punished, so I told myself. Dark-haired, shy Alice Walker and solidly built, blonde Nellie Leach, another fairly quiet character – qualities gained perhaps because each came from families with older brothers to ensure good behaviour – were soon drawn into the plot hatching in my brain. Alice would play Snow White and Nellie could have the role of Cinderella provided they were my partners in crime. And so the tip was visited and joy of joys, we brought home an old black kettle. Despite missing half of its spout, it experienced a dazzling though brief life as a magic lamp.

Weeks of the summer break from school honed the rehearsals and one Sunday afternoon we decided upon opening night.

With the stage a patch of earth Mother would use later to grow potatoes (Father definitely did not have green fingers) and the backcloth the air raid shelter, the grand event began.

Aladdin, dressed in a pair of brown lisle stockings, a yellow blouse donated by Hilda and a cardboard coolie hat made by Mother, asked loudly why he should go anywhere with Abanazer. The wicked wizard was played by raven-haired Olga Griffiths. Like the others, she lived a few doors along from us and, though she was younger than the rest of the cast, her dark hair seemed eminently suited to the role of Abanazer. Olga took great delight in the part, especially when she rubbed both hands together and declared pompously, ''Cos I can give you a lotta money.'

So the panto progressed. Denied permission to attend the royal ball Cinderella sang, 'Somewhere Over the Rainbow' while two mis-matched dwarves – all we could recruit – circled Snow White chanting 'Hi ho, hi ho, it's off to work we go'. In between Aladdin's bride exchanging an old lamp for a new one (which incidentally was Mother's aluminium teapot), Jack planted his beans and Red Riding Hood borrowed Widow Twanky's basket to take goodies to Grandmother.

So involved were we in a production devised and performed solely for our own entertainment, no audience was dreamed of. It certainly resembled nothing like a professional piece of theatre and there were no refreshments – wartime rationing, remember. So, each playing our part, singing songs no doubt badly out of tune, none of us noticed each bedroom window of every house in sight was open, neighbours and their families, my parents and sisters, all leaning out to catch every word and action.

II

A Job for Life

It was, I think, 1937 when Newman's Tube Works opened a factory at the junction of Holyhead Road and Dangerfield Lane. Father applied for a job and was employed. He worked there until his death aged sixty-four.

The benefit of Father at last securing full-time employment was, of course, felt financially. By no means an extravagant wage – work being scarce and the numbers of men on the dole being large meant a take-it-or-leave-it situation – it did not provide a rags-to-riches turnabout to life in 51 Dangerfield Lane, but it did ease the old problem of where the next meal was going to come from. To this could be added the extra pleasure of not seeing the look of defeat on Father's face and the shadow of worry on Mother's when, after hours of tramping from factory to factory and from town to town, he would return home still with no promise of a job.

This, then, was a new beginning and, although his working day was long and the hours away from home increased with the outbreak of the Second World War, he still continued the practice begun very early in our lives.

We would wait eagerly for the evening meal to be finished, sitting expectantly on the floor of the living room wondering what story would we be given to-night?

The living room was not large and the space allotted to each became more and more restricted as friends and playmates asked if they could join in. Mother's reply was always the same: 'Tell your mother where you be an' then you can come.' And come they did, in numbers.

Mother and Father being the most sociable of people, no one, young or old, was turned from their door. I often say that 51 Dangerfield Lane was the first social centre in Wednesbury and certainly during those awful years of war, had a bomb landed on it then half the population of the town might have found their new homes in Paradise!

Luckily this did not happen and for a couple of hours each evening – air raids allowing – we enjoyed this special time.

To the modern youngster this would seem horrendous or at best a waste of time. More lessons after school? What a turn off! But for us those hours spent with our parents were precious and the memory of them still is.

Each evening a different member of the group would be allowed to choose a subject to begin the proceedings. Mine, of course, was English. I hoped for a tale of Arthur and his Knights of the Round Table, Dick Turpin and his horse Black Bess, or maybe Charles II hiding in the oak tree in the grounds of Moseley Hall before escaping via Wednesbury's Trotters Lane, taking the route along Hawke's Lane and West Bromwich Black Lake and on eventually to the coast. These streets, so well known to us, brought the stories to life for me, and tales were Mother's department.

Father's English took the form of what he termed 'a spellin' B'. I never have known what the 'B' stood for but given my own twenty-five years of teaching children of ages seven to eleven I realise now how difficult were some of the words he chose: pneumonia, phlegm, nasturtium, photograph. None was easy to the young, but the effort made in order to get it right next time stood us in good stead.

The ten minutes given to this was followed by ten minutes of geography. 'Name the largest rivers in England. In which country is Lake Victoria?' Then came a quiz based upon history: 'Who was Ethelred the Unready? Which monarch ruled after George IV? What was the relationship of Kaiser Wilhelm II to the British royal family?' Follow this with the same amount of time spent grappling with mental arithmetic – at which Father was exceptionally good – and you would think us kids ready to cry 'Enough'. But no, we were ready for the next lesson.

Reading. Now, I liked this almost as much as I liked listening to stories and was always eager for my turn to read a passage selected from the newspaper, books being one of the many items our household budget did not yet stretch to. Next we would choose to recite a poem, or in the case of Joan and myself, who were perhaps too young to have learned any, a nursery rhyme. One of these affords my earliest memory of school.

I was four years old and it was my first day in the infant class. The teacher, Miss Knowles, asked could anyone recite a poem? That was my cue to show off. I was on that stage-like platform before she had time to blink, confidently piping out the words, 'There was an old woman who lived in a shoe.'

There must have been evenings when Mother felt like the character in that nursery rhyme with so many neighbours' children as well as her own stuffed into her living room like sardines in a can, but she never complained, not even when Father announced, 'now for some physical jerks'.

I developed no real liking for P.E. during my school years and when in the Seniors certainly did my utmost to avoid it, but at home, with Father as the instructor, I positively enjoyed it. With Mother watching from a chair wisely pushed to one corner we would mark time. This involved running on the spot. Next would be 'trunk forward bend'. Here we would bend from the waist to place hands flat on the floor. After a series of similar exercises would come the point we all liked best. Skirts caught between our legs and tucked into our waistbands and knicker legs we were ready for the highlight of the evening. Standing in line, we waited in turn to vault head over heels, our feet resting against the pantry door.

Years later, a childhood friend of Ann's, grown and married by the time Mother left Dangerfield Lane, became the next tenant of Number 51.

I wonder, Connie, do you sometimes recall those times you spent with Ann and her sisters, when you enthusiastically joined in those 'physical jerks'?

Meg's War

The words, 'This country is at war with Germany' had meant nothing at all to me at six years old. Life was as it had always been, going to school then back home to play in the Lane until Father's shrill whistle summoned us to get washed before bed.

But gradually things began to change. Mother, harassed as she was from managing on housekeeping money always spent days before the next instalment was due, wore an ever more worried look each morning she sent us off to school, waving from the gate until we were out of sight.

Almost sixty years on, it is nigh impossible to realise the fears of mothers for their families; who knew if they would see them safe again? It must have been a constant battle to prevent these fears spilling over, a battle which one day Mother lost.

Afternoon school for Junior children ended at four o'clock while the Seniors went on until four thirty. Ordered by Mother to wait for Phoebe to walk me home, I was allowed to help tidy the classroom after the rest of Miss Knowles' pupils had left. This was the part of the school day I most enjoyed and I would perform any task diligently. One afternoon, however, I must have been a bit too ardent for when tidying the nature table I knocked over a fish-paste jar holding water and buttercups. I felt more fright on seeing the stain of water seep into the white cloth, the small golden flowers strewn in a heap, than any I had experienced when air-raid sirens sounded. What could I say? What would Miss Knowles say? It had been an accident, but at the tender age of six logic had no place in my mind. Miss Knowles had not been in the classroom, she had not witnessed my misdemeanour! In the maelstrom of thought I spotted the school cat. Thus began my first excursion into the fields of deception. If I made myself scarce maybe she would assume the cat had tipped over the fish-paste jar.

A perfect match for any Olympic sprinter, I was out of that classroom and halfway along Holyhead Road before stopping for breath. The air-raid warning must have sounded yet no place in my memory records it, only the fact of a lovely sunlit afternoon, a strangely silent world where I was the only occupant. No person on the street, no traffic on the road, just myself, a child in her own safe, pleasant world.

But the world was no longer safe nor, in the next few moments, particularly pleasant. The drone first caught my attention and as it hummed closer I stood scanning the sky for some wonder. Could it be a dragon? I had read of such in books, maybe this was one of them.

A ripple of excitement shivering along my spine, I caught a glimpse of my dragon: wings spread, it glided grey and large out of the sunlight. There the fantasy was interrupted by the screech of tyres and a figure hurled itself upon me, pushing me facedown against the wall of the railway bridge, completely covering me from the hail of bullets which spat the length of the road. My dragon was a German bomber. Its bombs already dispatched, it was spraying bullets at the lorry my protector had been driving.

A lucky escape. Having told the man where I lived, I was driven home.

'Is this yoh'r babby?' My rescuer glared at Mother, hurrying down the side path and around to the front garden gate. What was a lorry doing here? No motor vehicle ever came – a horse and cart yes, but no motor!

'Is this yoh'r babby?'

The man lifted me from the cab.

Mother's expression of enquiry became one of anxiety. Snatching open the gate she stepped onto the footpath where I was still being held and now her green eyes flashed their danger signal. This man had hold of one of her kids and if he knew what was good for him he would let go of her right now!

'Leave 'er go!' The words were quiet though the warning behind them rang loud. 'Leave 'er go . . . now!'

Once the man released me, I was grabbed by Mother, the ferocious grip of her left hand biting into my shoulder.

'It be all right, missis, I wouldn't never 'urt no baby.'

He had read a sudden new fear showing behind Mother's stare. 'But yoh wants to look after 'er, next time them bloody Jerries decides to shed a few bullets then 'er might not be so lucky.'

Her hand still fast on my shoulder Mother listened to all the man had to say. Apology and thanks tumbling out together, she watched the lorry drive away.

A happy conclusion? Not for me!

Explanation ended, retribution began. Relief at my narrow escape might have been the emotion behind every smack but that did not ease the sting to my bottom!

Further into the war it became compulsory to carry your gas mask everywhere you went, and that included school. Older now, and finding school less than exciting, I trod the fields of deception more widely.

Each morning, following hand and handkerchief inspection, registration and prayer assembly, came gas-mask inspection. Each class returned from the hall to its own room where the teacher would conduct the inspection.

Got the picture?

This was an opportunity to reduce the hours of being cooped up and I grasped it with enthusiasm.

Morning after morning my cardboard box was missing, each time with a fresh excuse and on each occasion I was sent home to fetch it. The long walk there and back was a delight, strategically timed so I returned to the classroom just minutes before dinner break.

This happy state of affairs lasted just so long. Being sent to the headmistress to explain was daunting, but still the escapade did not quite end. I was becoming adept in the art of deception, and forgetting the gas mask was too good a skive to give up.

I might have gone on trying to pull the wool over the teacher's eyes but the second visit to the head-mistress's room resulted in the ultimatum, 'The box or your Mother'. She would see one or the other in school the very next morning. I knew that was the end. I might fool the staff of St James' but I could not fool Mother! Both box and mask dutifully arrived each day after that.

One of Mother's regular sayings was, 'What you

lose on the swings you gain on the roundabout.' This was certainly so in the case of the gas mask. I had lost that precious hour or so free of the classroom, only to have it returned – sometimes – courtesy of the Luftwaffe.

Bombing raids, an almost standard night-time feature, became a more regular daytime interruption. If they took place while coming from or going to school, then official instruction stated you take cover in the nearest shelter. Again, my innocence saw this as another great way of staying free of school and I took advantage of it on every occasion which presented itself. There could be no displeasure voiced by teachers, especially since the school had no specific form of bomb shelter for quite some time.

One early morning memory of an air raid during school hours is of long lines of children being led across the street to St James' Church and there shepherded into what I can only hope were cellars.

To this day I remember the utter darkness as a door shut away the light and in that complete blackness the sound of a teacher's hands clapping together and her voice calling, 'Look this way, girls.'

How were we supposed to know in which direction to look? I've never yet fathomed that out.

Fortunately that didn't happen too often. Some half mile or so away, Holyhead Road Council

School eventually had air-raid shelters erected and we were invited to share. With any weekday raid the entire school population trotted this distance along a road serving a number of factories, all engaged in the production of munitions and therefore the target for German bombers, but hazardous as that journey was it was infinitely preferable to the Church cellars.

There are many memories of those wartime years locked away inside all of us; enough, I would imagine, for each of you reading this to write a book full of them, but this one I would like to share.

Ann, three years older than me, was, along with myself, found by the 'nit nuss' to have contracted impetigo. The consequence of this was a quick march to Albert Street Clinic where our hair was cropped so short it was the original crewcut. No parental consultation, no 'We think it advisable', just down to the clinic and off with the lot. The 'lot' being hair which reached to our bottoms, you can imagine Mother's shock when her daughters returned home like freshly shorn sheep, our scalps dotted with gentian violet, which I can only suppose was an antiseptic. Mother's visit to Albert Street Clinic? I leave that to your imagination.

For Ann, the trauma of being virtually bald was too much. She took refuge in her Girl Guide hat. Night and day pulled as low on her ears as was physically possible, wherever Ann went the hat went too, even to bed. No problem. Until the night of one heavy raid.

We were awakened by Mother telling us not to wait to get dressed but to run to the shelter – every house had its own by this time. She grabbed Joan, the youngest of three in a bed, and called Ann and myself to follow. But Germans or no Germans, Ann was going nowhere without her hat. It had been placed in its usual overnight position on the knob of the brass bedstead but in the scramble it had fallen off. The throb throb of enemy planes passing overhead made no impression on Ann. No hat, no shelter! Mother's repeated calls went unheeded as the two of us tried to find the elusive headgear. The fact we could use no light meant this was a process of touch – a process brought to an abrupt end with the arrival of Father. The gentlest of men, he had never raised hand or voice to any of us, so it came as a serious shock when he caught us by the scruff of the neck, hauling us downstairs and out of the house.

But Ann wasn't finished. The hat heaven had seen fit to slip into her hand at the very last moment now safely on her head, she was about to step into the air-raid shelter when the sky overhead exploded. 'Ooh,' exclaimed Ann, 'ooh, ain't that pretty!' That was the very moment Father's boot helped her take cover, for the 'pretty fireworks' were what were locally termed 'basket bombs', the official description being incendiary bombs. The hat? Hitler at his worst did not succeed in separating Ann from that. It did long and excellent service in the months it took to re-grow her crowning glory.

13

Father Goes to War

Having been invalided out of the First World War because of breathing problems caused by a broken nose suffered in the unit boxing ring, Father was exempt from World War Two and served in the Home Guards. But as a young child I did not understand that. To me the uniform of the Home Guard was that of any other soldier, and soldiers went away and didn't come home!

Based in an upper storey room of Newman's Tube factory, fire watch and Home Guard duties were undertaken by volunteers until a regular Home Guard unit was formed in Darlaston and Wednesbury.

This voluntary unit, all from the neighbourhood, took turns at these various duties. Now I can't speak of others, but Father, he seemed to arrange his shift to suit the licensing hours.

His local, the relatively recently built Highgate Arms, known to its regular patrons as 'the new un', was just a couple of streets away from home and mere yards from Newman's Tube Works. This meant it was an ideal position for enjoying a drink and a game of cards between finishing a twelve and a half hour working day and beginning a stint of lookout duty.

In the first months of the war, all of this was unknown to me. On those evenings Father was home just long enough to wash and eat a meal. I was just told that 'Daddy has to work over'. This worked well until the arrival of the khaki uniform.

It was Saturday, and that meant the younger members of the family could stay up that extra hour. Years later Mother would laugh and say she wished she had put me to bed, it would have avoided the crying match she had to contend with that night.

When I was called to the back porch to receive a goodnight kiss before Father left to return to the factory to 'work over' there was just enough light peeping from the kitchen to show he was 'a soldier'.

Hysterics is a mild way to describe what happened next.

Kids at school had talked of older brothers being called up, the tears of mothers and young wives, the worried faces when the postman didn't call. All because the Army had taken their loved ones. Now it was taking mine, the father I adored.

Now, if there was anything designed to destroy Father, it was seeing any of his wenches in tears.

'Bugger 'Itler,' he declared, 'and bugger the 'Ome Guard, I'll goo when my babbies be asleep.'

Father led the way into the house, me wailing in his arms, Mother carried Joan, who was sobbing in sympathy. That was the last any of us saw of the uniform.

Not until a couple of years later did I learn the truth of those civil defence hours. One Sunday afternoon, Mother deemed me old enough to accompany Father, as volunteers by that time served only in the capacity of 'fire watcher'. I was so full of self importance I could hardly climb the stairs to that upstairs room. I was going to help my dad fight the war!

Fight is not quite the word. The room was large and filled with sunlight. In the centre was a table with enamel mugs and a tin kettle, while at the end furthest from the door was a set of bunks of the type issued for use in garden air-raid shelters.

'Up yoh goo, mah babby.'

Father lifted me onto the topmost bunk and handed me a book of fairy tales Mother had bought the day before at a jumble sale, then he stretched out on the lower bunk and snored until his replacement arrived to take over!

But, despite this relaxed approach, the volunteers were still prepared, should need arise, to do just that little bit extra.

Father Goes to War

1941 was a dark period of the war. Nights spent in air-raid shelters had parents edgy, mothers worried children might be caught up in raids on the way to or from school, fathers fearing for the safety of families. But despite this, Mother never lost the spirit of hospitality. Anyone calling at her door was welcome, including a young man who came asking for a drink of water.

True to form, he was invited in and asked to sit down while a pot of tea was brewed. Having followed my own usual habit of defying the rule of remaining on school premises for the whole of midday break I was in the kitchen. I was surprised when Mother sent me to get sugar from the pantry and followed me there. I was even more surprised when she whispered, 'Go fetch your daddy. Tell 'im to come now!'

There was never any mistaking the times Mother was not prepared for argument or question. This was one of those times. Calling loudly that I would be late for school unless I left immediately, I ran hell for leather to Newman's Tube Works. Having delivered the message, there was no way I was going to miss the outcome and it proved well worth the telling-off I received from the headmistress for a) leaving school grounds and b) being late for registration.

Father arrived with three workmates. The young man, still sitting in Mother's kitchen, was asked his business. Remember, everyone in the area knew everyone else and a stranger asking his way inevitably gave rise to suspicion – particularly this stranger, with his 'funny' accent. Convincing though his replies may have been, they were not satisfactory to Father.

Ordering the man into the street, they formed a square with him at the centre. Then, in perfect 'Dad's Army' style, positioned in the middle of the road, they shouldered rifles containing not a single bullet and, still in the roadway, ignoring whatever traffic might gather behind, marched their prisoner to the police station.

Months afterwards word was 'accidentally' dropped by the local bobby. Mother's guest had proved to be a German spy.

An amusing story? Yes. But war has two faces and this was only one of them.

By daylight and nighttime, enemy bombing raids had increased in number and intensity. People were weary in mind and body. Father was no exception. Having followed his day of factory labour with a couple of hours of fire watch, which by this stage of events was taken very seriously, he and the rest of the family were in bed when sirens sounded the alarm. First reaction was to wait: not every raid reached our part of the Midlands. But Mother felt this was going to be a 'bad un' and it was definitely coming our way.

Calling for us to get dressed, she hurried downstairs. Hilda, Phoebe and Ann followed, quickly assisting in the gathering of coats, shoes and the rough battleship grey Army blankets each family had been issued for use in the shelter, and which had to be dried and aired daily because of the damp rising constantly from the ground, and condensation dripping down the corrugated-metal sheets that formed its walls and roof.

Of Joan and myself, there was no sign. Father had collected us and was back in bed, a child snuggled in each arm, and there he stayed firmly refusing pleas to come to the shelter. He had had enough, declaring that 'No bits o' tin will stand a bomb, so if we'm goin' to die we'll die in bed!' He remained where he was.

Some memories remain clear and strong all through life. That night, for me, is one of those memories.

The night had become alive with sound. The sky vibrated like a nest of gigantic, angry wasps. Neighbours' calls and cries as they ran for their shelters echoed Mother's own fear: this was going to be a 'bad un'. But call as she might Father was not moving.

In the distance, the thud of striking bombs brought a strange calm to the mêlée. Neighbours ceased their cries, their only calls now an answer to the air-raid warden's, 'Everybody all right?'

Mother however was far from all right. Three children would not leave the house without her and she would not leave without her other two and her husband. With Mr Siveter's shout of 'Everythin' all right, George?' she asked his help in getting Father to come downstairs. Needless to say it did not work.

It might seem from reading this that Father was a stubborn-minded man, but in truth he was the opposite. He would bend over backwards to suit other people and in all his years he was not once known to threaten another person. Patience and good manners were central to his way of life; except that night.

The tether stretched to its limit, his reply to Mr Siveter's threat to come to fetch us two children was, 'Come up then, Jim, an' I'll throw you back down them bloody stairs!'

Impasse had been reached. At least, it had until the arrival of the local policeman. There was no beating about the bush, no modern-day psychological approach of 'We can talk this thing through', and no stand-off allowing time to do the job for him.

Standing at the foot of the stairs, he bellowed, 'George, you'd better come down. Annie and the kids be frightened, it don't tek no tellin', they needs you with them; if you decides to stop in bed then you can do that but it means Annie and her kids remainin' in the house, they won't budge without you.'

Father's resistance crumbled. In minutes we were all together in the shelter, joined with the Harris and Timmins families, neighbours who from the first air raid had made regular practice of sharing with us despite the cramped conditions. We were with friends; they were not alone in their fear.

That was one of the longest raids I remember. All through the night wave after wave of enemy aircraft filled our world with fear. Her two youngest with heads held close into her side, the three older ones grouped near, Mother sat with her neighbours listening to the whistle of bombs, holding her breath for those seconds between the whistle ending and the shuddering thump of a strike.

Dawn settled into morning, but though the bombardment had eased the danger was not yet over. Longing for a cigarette, Father drew aside the sacking – the only cover to the entrance of the shelter – and climbed out. He said later that the sky in the distance was on fire. He called to each of the surrounding gardens to ascertain the safety of yet other neighbours entrenched in shelters, then he lit the cigarette. At that precise moment, something struck the line prop next to him.

Infuriated at the behaviour of 'daft kids', he shouted angrily, 'Don't you think we be goin' through enough without you silly buggers throwin' bibbles!'

It was a few hours before a second siren sounded the 'all clear' and Father found the 'bibble' which had so very narrowly missed his head. The stone he thought hurled by 'daft kids' proved to be a large ragged piece of metal, part of an incendiary bomb found at the bottom of our garden.

Bomb casing and shrapnel. They sat on the kitchen shelf for many years after the war had ended.

Trophies and memories!

Trophies were eventually abandoned and faded from mind. But memories, though faint, and old hurts forgiven, will never be entirely erased.

14

Lessons of a Different Kind

After the incident of the German bomber, augmented by Mother's threat of retributions, I took to waiting for Ann before coming home from school. Now an eight-year-old member of the Junior School, I thought this all a bit much, I could go home by myself for heaven's sake! But then the risk of German bombers was nothing, should I arouse Mother's wrath a second time.

During the warm days of summer, standing alone in the playground could become a pain in the rear. After all, I could be home, deep in some game with Peter, my best of all friends. This frustration never seemed so bad on Friday afternoons, for the final lesson for some of the Seniors was music. Listening to them sing, their voices floating into the quiet, sunlit playground, was a pure pleasure, one where the earth stood still to share the moment. Friday after Friday I stood, having chased away any other child daring to believe they might also remain to listen to that delightful singing; when I was in the 'big school' I too would learn those songs!

Inevitably summer turned to winter, golden sunshine gave way to pewter skies and rain and I could no longer wait in the playground until Ann's school day ended so we could go home together.

I was given permission to wait the half hour in the corridor outside Ann's classroom. It was mind-blowingly dull, until I heard of 'Abu-ben-Adam'.

From first hearing that name, I was entranced. But plead as I might, Ann would not take the bother of enlightening me. Once school was over for the day, she wanted no more to do with it; Abu-ben-Adam was lost to me.

The following week, the name reached out to me again. It pushed aside the barrier of classroom walls and scooped me up, holding me in the magic of those words. There and then I vowed that on becoming a Senior School pupil I would learn all there was to know of that intriguing, enticing 'Abu'.

As it happened, I did not have to wait another three years. Hoping each week to renew brief, all too quickly gone moments, I listened intently whenever that hope was realised. Sitting in that corridor, I learned by heart what was never taught in the time I was in Senior School.

The songs sung by the girls of Mrs Hadley's class

have long disappeared from my memory but 'Abu' still remains loved now not only by that eight-year-old girl but by her daughters and their children.

'Tell it again, Mom.'

'Say it again, Grandma.'

I've heard those words so many times, yet the enjoyment of fulfilling the request has never diminished. Abu-ben-Adam still imparts to me a calm, peaceful serenity. In the hope that it will give the same to you, I reproduce it now.

Abu-ben-Adam
A poem by Leigh Hunt

Abu-ben-Adam, may his tribe increase,
Awoke one night from a deep dream of peace,
And saw within the moonlight in his room
Making it rich and like a lily in bloom,
An angel writing in a book of gold,
Exceeding peace had made ben Adam bold,
And to the Presence in the room he said,
'What writest thou?'
The vision raised its head and with a look
Made of all sweet accord answered,
'The names of those who love the Lord.'
'And is mine one?' said Abu.
'Nay, not so,' replied the angel.
Abu spake more low but cheerily still and said,

'I pray thee then, write me as one who loves his
fellow men.'
The angel wrote and vanished.
Next night it came again with great awakening
light
And showed the names whom love of God had
blessed.
And lo,
ben Adam's name led all the rest.

Childhood is marred by any war and those lived
during the Second World War proved so for many.
But not every trauma can be placed upon Hitler's
doorstep; one which still brings a shiver to my blood
most certainly could not.

Though 1943 saw parents deeply concerned for
the safety of children during air raids, it was thought
safe enough for them to play outdoors for a couple of
hours after school and at weekends. One such weekend I asked if my cousin Mary and myself could have
a picnic.

One slice each of bread and margarine and a bottle
of water being the only goodies available, we set off,
warned by Father not to go near the canal. The
council-owned allotments were only yards from the
front door of Number 51 Dangerfield Lane, so that
was Mother's proposed venue for the picnic. But
where was the adventure in that? Needless to say,

the allotments got the thumbs down from both Mary and me.

Separated from Dangerfield Lane by the Holyhead Road was a large expanse of ground left derelict after a button-making factory had burned down a few years previously. Some way back from this ran the canal, which served a large chemical works, the fumes of which were deemed by locals to 'be good for the chest'. Father once took me inside the works where a friendly watchman allowed him to hold me over a vat of strong-smelling liquid in order to cure a bronchial cough.

The chemical works did not tempt Mary and me on that gentle sun-filled Sunday afternoon, but the canal did.

Nearing the bridge that spanned the waters we soon became aware of the reason Father had said not to go there. A group of lads were using the parapet as a diving platform. Some small, others not so small, they were all stark naked.

Two giggling ten-year-old girls made their way quickly further along the towpath.

From the spot we chose to sit, we could still see the bridge and its occupants, but now more discreetly. An hour or so later, the sandwiches still a treat to come, I noticed a figure approaching from the direction of the bathers. For some unknown reason the sight made me edgy. The closer the figure came the more my spine tingled until at last I said I thought we should go home. Mary laughed at the cause of my sudden desire to end our pleasant afternoon; it was only a young man out for a Sunday afternoon walk, she said.

But that was not all the man was out for. A strong sense of foreboding had me on my feet. At that same moment the man broke into a run catching Mary before she could move. Already some yards away, I heard her cries and turning back saw the man had her caught in one arm while his other hand was inside her knickers. Fortunately our combined screams had the swimmers racing toward us but not before the man let Mary fall and ran away in the direction of the chemical works.

Speaking for myself I had never been warned about what are today termed paedophiles and I have no hesitation in saying that Mary had received no such warning either. Nothing of the sort was, it seemed, heard of in our corner of the world. Yet for some unknown reason, watching that man approach had my nerves on edge. An early example of feminine intuition? Maybe.

From a feeling of guilt that we had done something far more terrible than ignoring Father's edict, Mary and I said nothing to our respective parents of what had happened; we did not speak of it to anyone, but held the fear and self-reproach locked inside.

At this juncture of the war, it was decided that in addition to collecting newspapers etc., to aid the war effort, children over the age of nine years should be taught the rudiments of first aid.

A good idea, agreed Mother and Aunt Phoebe – Mary's mother – and so we were enrolled. The evening of our first tuition arrived and off we went. The teaching was to be given in a small building in Pinfold Street, Darlaston, and truth to tell, we were looking forward to this new venture. Imagine our horror when the first-aid instructor turned out to be none other than the man from the towpath.

First-aid lessons began and ended that same evening! Mother did not press for reasons. Could this have been due to Hilda, now seventeen, attending the same course for only two weeks? Mother did not always require to have things explained in words of one syllable.

Our garden production of Cinderella might have been amusing but it could not match the colour and spectacle, the sheer heady excitement of the pantomime being staged at the Grand Theatre in Wolverhampton. To us, however, this could only be a dream.

Mother's youngest sister, widowed in her early twenties, had chosen to return to the parental home in Pitt's Square and later to move with William Henry and Mary Ann when, in their turn, they were given a newly built council house in Margaret Road, a two or three minute walk from our house in Dangerfield Lane.

Some years later, after a second marriage to Evan, who was employed by Guest, Keen and Nettlefold engineering works, and with financial assistance from Grandfather, whose home they still shared, Aunt Phoebe enjoyed a less economically stressful life.

Having been sent to Granddad's on some errand or other, Ann was told by Aunt Phoebe of a treat in store: Mary – the child of her first marriage – and Ann could go to see the pantomime, provided she had the necessary tram fare and money to buy her theatre ticket.

Excitement shining in her face, Ann raced home with the news. As can be guessed, Mother's purse was empty, but why not take the bottles back? suggested Nanny Harris. Next door, Mr Harris liked his beer brought to the house, one or other of us kids being sent on this nightly errand. It was the practice at that time for pubs, off licences and shops to put a premium on bottled beer and soft drinks, this being refunded on return of the bottles. Tuppence and sometimes threepence for each container ensured they were always returned.

Ann needed no further advice. Mr Harris was a kindly soul and his wife was like a grandmother to us. The bottles were given and Ann raced the length of the Lane, returning some to Bartrum's off licence, some to the Duke of York public house, and – in the case of a couple of Tizer lemonade bottles – to Patty Longmore's grocery shop in Banfield Road.

One shilling and fourpence! Surely that would be enough.

Washed, dressed in the clean frock meant for school next day, hair brushed and braided at Mother's insistence, Ann at last was off to see Cinderella. For her the dream was almost a reality.

Almost!

Hurrying towards the bend where Margaret Road joined Dangerfield Lane, Ann heard voices in the darkness. Wartime meant no street lighting but she recognised the people: Aunt Phoebe, Uncle Evan and cousin Mary, they were obviously coming to meet her.

Except they were not!

They walked straight past, and with them was Hilda Bassett. Another child had taken Ann's place.

Disappointment too strong for anything but tears, Ann sat on the pavement and sobbed.

When she heard of what had happened, Mother took the one shilling and fourpence and placed it on the shelf above the fireplace. Ann was put to bed with the rest of us.

Although there had been no more bottles waiting to be returned, the next day the coins on the shelf were added to.

Father's one decent pair of trousers and jacket now resided in Shaw's pawnshop.

Ann would realise her dream.

Mother was no doubt hurt by her sister taking the daughter of a friend to see that pantomime in place of Ann, but it was never referred to. Mother was too forgiving a character. Ann and I, on the other hand, still discuss it, both of us coming to the conclusion that, though clean, Ann's clothing was not of a standard suitable for Aunt Phoebe, who dressed Mary in frilly dresses and pretty shoes.

She would have known that the money for Ann's ticket would be difficult to come by and, as a result, take some time to acquire; time which beforehand must have been given to Mrs Bassett in order to have her own daughter washed and dressed for the special occasion. And time for them all to have left before Ann could return.

An act of spite or just thoughtlessness? Hilda and Phoebe champion the second. In their younger days, spent in Pitt's Square, Aunt Phoebe had played with them, been like an older sister in her treatment of them, but with the birth of Mary (close on the heels of my own birth) her attitude towards Ann, myself and eventually Joan, became ever more dismissive – the kindest word I can apply – until neither of us would happily run an errand to Grandad's house.

15

Growing Pains

Growing up in Dangerfield Lane in the thirties and forties meant learning to tek yoh'r own part'. In effect, that meant being prepared to fight your own battles. This was especially so where a family consisted of girls with no brother to fight for them. So learn we all did, and each put that learning into practice at the drop of a hat – or at the few times Mother was slighted or called a 'cripple' the perpetrator paying dearly for the crime.

Such payment was extracted by Hilda. At fourteen, almost at the end of her school life, she was walking home with one of the Bladen boys. Billy's boasting was of the 'we are better than you' type. Taller and heavier than her companion, Hilda found herself growing more and more scathing as Billy's claims became more and more excessive. Finally she told him to 'Stop trying to be what you are not! Everybody knows you've got no more than anybody else in the Lane!'

This shot across the bows brought Billy to a halt.

No wench was going to get the better of him! His face dark with fury, he looked at the girl facing him and spat, 'An' all the Lane knows I don't 'ave no cripple for a mother!'

Billy regretted uttering those words. He would say years afterward he didn't know what had hit him, but the bruises stayed long after that tigress left him with his head stuck between the bars of a fence. She gave a final kick to his bottom and left him to the mercy of any passerby for rescue.

It was not just Mother we rose in defence of. An unspoken rule existed among the five of us kids, 'Touch one and you touch them all!'

It came into play when Ann was threatened by another lad living a few doors from us in the Lane. Now Ann was lippy, her tongue often got her into trouble and this it seemed was just one of those times.

Whatever the cause, it had Dickie Deeley chasing after her as Ann took to her heels. Shouting 'I'm goin' to punch yer lights out', he eventually grabbed Ann's coat and pulled her to the ground.

The first blow landed on Ann's back, the second on the side of her attacker's head.

Phoebe had arrived on the scene!

The ensuing battle was furious but decisive. There would be no more threat from that quarter. Dickie had learned what others had learned before him and others would learn after him.

'Don't mess with the Astbury girls, they take no truck from anybody.'

'Touch one and you touch them all.'

This rule is still recognised among us sisters; each rises swiftly in defence of the others, though not, I stress, with the fisticuffs of youth.

Childhood, and even teen years, held no such reservations, and the age of the aggressor made no impression.

Miss Patrick was headmistress of the Junior department of St James' Church of England School. Dark-haired and dumpy of figure, she seemed always to wear a neckline that stopped just short of her breasts. This was a magnet for young eyes for whenever something displeased her – and it often did – a red flush would rise from that covered chest and travel along her neck and into her face; a volcano beginning to erupt.

Erupt it did one day. We were being taught the skills of knitting. Now, I wasn't the sharpest pin in the cushion. I didn't realise that you had to knit the last stitch on the needle before turning about. Watching the brief exhibition of some half dozen stitches being knitted before the piece was handed back to me I proceeded to knit back along the needle. This was too much for the headmistress who had come into the classroom to check progress. Snatching needles and wool from my hands she rolled up my cardigan sleeve and slapped my arm hard.

I never told Mother of this. The years passed and I entered the Senior School, in the upper rooms of the same building. But though I moved on the resentment of that unfair punishment remained. The youngest of Mother's brood, Joan, was now in the Juniors. One day a friend of mine, Pamela Harris, came rushing to me in the Senior's playground; 'Miss Patrick is going to slap your little 'un for runnin' in the corridor!'

She hadn't gasped the last word before I was in that classroom facing an astonished – and very angry – headmistress.

'You go outside,' I told a frightened Joan. I turned to the red-faced teacher, 'You leave our babby alone!'

Morning break ended. Lessons resumed. Five minutes later a young child entered the classroom. Could Miss Patrick see Margaret Astbury?

Down I went to that other classroom, where some forty or so open-mouthed kids waited for the show. The chest was red, the neck and face scarlet. Announcing loudly she would not be spoken to in such fashion by a child, Miss Patrick proceeded to roll up my sleeve. Then, as one hand held my arm and the other rose to strike, I looked her calmly in the eyes and said, 'Hit me, go on. Hit me an' our mother'll be down 'ere this afternoon.'

I did not receive the threatened slap.

Nor did I tell Mother of that little contretemps. Why not? Because I was more afraid of her reaction than I had been of Miss Patrick. I had rushed into that classroom without stopping to think. Would Mother understand, or would she view my behaviour as rudeness and thus deliver her own form of punishment? Walking home at lunchtime I warned Joan not to tell.

I think Miss Patrick too must have thought the same, for there the matter rested.

It is said we only remember the good things of life, perhaps because we don't want to recall the less pleasant. But these happened too, regardless of the cause.

Ann was in the Senior School. Arriving late one morning she followed the system decreed and waited in the cloakroom with several other late arrivers. The entire upper school was at assembly, the classrooms and corridors empty of children and teachers. For Ann, fretting at the consequence of arriving late, the singing of hymns and recital of prayers seemed never ending. With the last Amen, the classes were dismissed and Ann joined the line of children returning to her own classroom.

Called to the teacher's desk, Ann thought to explain the reason for her lateness by placing the blame on the delayed arrival of the bus, but this morning Miss Willetts was in no mood for excuses.

'Stand there!'

Ann was waved to one side of the tall-windowed room while another child was despatched with a message asking for every child who had arrived late that morning be sent to Miss Willetts' room.

What was going on? Ann expected the customary lecture and one hundred lines, but there was nothing; even instruction for the morning lesson had not been given. Sensing an eruption the class sat with wide eyes and bated breath.

With the arrival of the other late children, the first rumbles of that threatened eruption began.

Which of them had arrived late first? How long before the others? Had they waited together the whole time? Had Ann come to the classroom before assembly ended?

The questions came rapidly, Miss Willetts' displeasure rising with each one, then red-faced with anger she slapped the desk with a ruler.

To a highly nervous Ann, the slight figure seemed to grow, the look on her face becoming the threat of doom.

Then came the thunderbolt.

On her arrival in the classroom that morning Miss Willetts had placed a threepenny piece on her desk. It had been there when she took the class into the hall for assembly. Now it was gone. Threepenny pieces could not get up and walk. Someone had stolen it, and the thief was one of the children who had come late. Of those, only Ann would have cause to come into this classroom, therefore it must have been she who had taken the money.

Protestation, tears, naught impressed the stony-faced Miss Willetts and certainly not the feelings of a ten-year-old girl.

When an order to empty her pockets produced no coin Ann was commanded to remove her shoes and socks. No 'lost' threepenny piece was revealed, so another child was sent to bring Ann's coat from the cloakroom. The money must be in her coat pocket. But that pocket too was empty.

All efforts at recovering her property having failed, Miss Willetts was forced to begin the morning lessons, her sharp movements and needle voice clear indications that all was not yet over.

At playtime, sisters Hilda and Phoebe were given no other reason for Ann's distress save, 'Teacher shouted at me for bein' late!' They remarked it was her own fault and rejoined their friends in the part of the tiny playground traditionally reserved for the top class, those pupils approaching leaving age.

Almost at the end of the morning. Miss Willetts looked up from the exercise books she was marking.

'I remember now,' she announced, the light of fury dying from her eyes. 'I gave the threepenny piece to my nephew for his birthday.'

That was it. No apology, no expression of regret for the distress her accusations had caused, the matter was over and done.

Not quite!

When we came home for the midday meal, Mother asked the reason for Ann's red puffy eyes.

'Her was late.' Hilda and Phoebe gave their garnered account. 'Her went the long way round, down Woden Road under the donkey bridge.'

The fact that this included crossing ground made treacherous by the tipping of slag from the furnaces of various steel-making factories and having to cross a busy railway goods line, would indeed account for her daughter's late arrival at school. But tears? There was more behind them than a ticking off for being late.

Mother demanded the truth and nothing but the truth. She listened to the whole sorry episode, made us wash our hands and faces and ushered us off back to school.

Some half hour into the afternoon session there came a knock at the classroom door. Mother had arrived.

Though her right arm could not lift of its own volition Mother's left arm had no such disability;

indeed, her hand seemed to have developed a compensatory strength.

'You accused my wench of stealin' . . .'

Mother's voice was calm, her face showing no sign of the wrath burning inside.

'It was a mistake, it is finished with.'

'Oh, it was a mistake all right!' Mother answered the slightly flustered teacher, 'but it be far from finished with!'

The words were hardly said before the unfortunate Miss Willetts found herself pulled from the step of her desk and flung backwards across a table, Mother's hand gripping the collar of her blouse.

'You called my daughter a thief, now let's see you call me one!'

Wide eyed, enthralled by the drama, the whole class breathed as one.

'Well, go on!'

The teacher's head remained against the table.

'Let's hear it. Or do you only 'ave courage enough to accuse a little 'un?'

Beneath Mother's hand the croaked reply, though indistinguishable to the spellbound class, must have been an apology, for Miss Willetts was released. But Mother's anger was not yet dissipated.

She waved a finger threateningly at the distinctly red face and said loudly, 'When any one of my daughters does anything they shouldn't, then they deserves all that they gets and more when they get 'ome. I don't claim to have raised no angels but I've raised no thief neither! Now I warns you, next time you loses a threepenny bit you be very careful who you accuse of tekin' it, for next time you won't be let up from that table in one piece!'

Assault by a parent? Nowadays such behaviour would result in legal action; sixty-three years ago, and perhaps fortunate for all concerned, it did not.

At the risk of becoming repetitive, I say again my parents were the most social of people, as has been attested to many times by folk who knew them. Friendliness and trust were bywords with both, but these attributes were sometimes taken advantage of.

A prime example of this followed the abdication of the uncrowned King Edward VIII. This was viewed as a catastrophe by many of the adult population and certainly caused regret to Mother and Father, but for those children attending St James' School it afforded a deal of excitement. There was a new king on the throne and soon there would be a coronation.

They of course would not witness the grand event – television for the Astbury family and many others was a long way into the future – but photographs in newspapers showed the soon-to-be-crowned George VI, Elizabeth his wife, equally to be crowned as queen, and of course their two children.

History lessons became heavily involved with tracing the lineage of the royal couple; geography, ever jingoistic, outlined the great British Empire, but the deepest impression made on young minds was descriptions of robes and coronets, of a golden coach drawn by white horses, jewel-encrusted crowns and of course long scarlet trains trimmed with ermine and held by satin-costumed page boys. Every fairytale ever heard, every picture of beautiful princesses and handsome princes, was brought vividly to life in fertile imaginations and though art lessons did not produce anything of the calibre of Frans Hals or Holbein, nor did paintings of fairytale princesses achieve the ethereal beauty that Alphonse Mucha painted, the results were placed on every classroom wall alongside similarly painted Union Jack flags. All of this, giving as much pleasure as it did, paled beside that next delight.

To mark this historic occasion, children in the Junior School were presented with a book depicting the coronation. A royal blue cover embossed with gold insignia was for Ann a gift from the gods. Holding it with care approaching reverence, protecting it beneath her coat, she carried it home.

Across the street, the H– children, attending a different school, had received no such book. In addition, one of them was suffering a bout of measles. This in no way perturbed Mother. 'Of course you can borrow it,' was her reply to Mrs H–'s request. Ann waited several days for her treasure to be returned, only to discover its cover ripped away, the pages crumpled and strewn across the road.

It is said you learn from experience but Mother did not learn, she simply allowed her friendly nature to lead her into repeating the same thing.

This time I was the recipient of a book. Achieving top marks in school examinations, I was awarded the accompanying prize.

As delighted as Ann had been, I carried it home, proudly showing Mother the illuminated certificate pasted on the inside of the cover.

. . . Presented to Margaret Rose Astbury . . .

Just as delighted I showed it to Father on his return from work, revelling in his praise. But delight was to be short lived. Once again a neighbour, this time Maisie S– of Banfield Road, borrowed it to show to her family. That was the last I ever saw of my prize.

Maybe it was not destroyed as Ann's book had been; perhaps one day I may still make the acquaintance of *John Halifax, Gentleman*.

Is it old habits die hard or that you can't teach an old dog new tricks? Either of these could in fairness be attributed to George and Annie, but their daughters know it was the same friendly attitude led yet again to folly.

This time it was Father. Meeting a sociable couple of men at the pub, he invited them home to meet the family. Well mannered and perfectly behaved they stayed for some time, then, on preparing to leave, the one who had been introduced simply as Roly asked if he could borrow the book lying on the table.

A week before, Mother had been again to the Pinfold Street chapel where jumble sales proved a regular event. At that one she had spent sixpence. Quite a sum seeing the same amount would buy a couple of duck eggs for Father and enough potatoes to make chips to feed the rest of us. But all such considerations went to the wall when she spotted a large, beautifully bound book fastened with brass clasps, brass triangles protecting each corner while the edges of the pages gleamed a soft gold. Her Margaret would adore that book. And so I did, for a week!

A volume of *Pilgrim's Progress*, the inside of the book was every bit as beautiful as the cover. Each page of the story was supported by a full-page illustration of some aspect of the text, exquisitely painted in gold, blues, red that shone from the paper as vividly as manuscripts of old, and each in turn was faced with a cover of silk tissue.

A treasure indeed. And one obviously recognised by the said Roly.

Readily accepting the word of his new-found friends that they'd return the book were they allowed to borrow it, Father agreed.

Like the hard-won prize of *John Halifax, Gentleman*, *Pilgrim's Progress* was never returned.

16

Mother Does Her Bit

At the ages of sixteen and fourteen respectively, Hilda and Phoebe were working at Springs and Pressings, a small factory in Darlaston. With Father also now in full-time employment at the recently opened Newman's Tubes, the family financial situation had eased. But the same could not be said of the war, that situation grew worse by the hour.

Nineteen forty-one found the country fighting for its life. Air raids were a constant occurrence, often lasting long into the night, which left people weary and depressed. Yet they still had to go to work. Each news bulletin telling of German advances, of further occupation of foreign territory and fear of invasion sat heavy in everybody's heart; this was a war Britain seemed set to lose.

The industrial Black Country, traditionally a place of coal-mining and steel-production, was of vital importance, which explained the barrage of air attacks. But the assault only served to strengthen the will of its people. Women and girls took jobs in light engineering, producing weapons and ammunition, while those men not eligible for, or exempt from, service in the armed forces took on more demanding work.

Some of this took place in the area's 'shadow' factories. Camouflaged so as to be unrecognisable from the air, their vast doors opened at night only after every light other than the muted ones absolutely necessary for guiding out the tanks and heavy armaments made there was extinguished, these factories were extremely 'hush hush'.

Every person who *could* work to produce the necessary tools of war did so. Including some maybe not so well suited . . .

It was at this time that Mother, who had never worked outside of the home in her life, decided she would do her bit for her country.

Situated on Pinfold Street near to Darlaston's Bull Stake and some half mile from our house, there opened a unit where disabled persons could work assembling various components needed in the construction of machinery vital to the war effort.

It was here that Mother saw her opportunity. Her crippled left leg and right arm were to be no deterrent.

'I don't think you should go out to work, you 'ave enough to do with the 'ouse and the kids.' Father tried to dissuade her. 'You probably won't like it anyway.'

'*Like*!' Mother countered sharply. 'If folk could do

only what they likes then it be quite probable 'Itler would be sittin' in Buckin'am Palace right now for ain't nobody *likes* goin' to war!'

Father relinquished his argument. Once his wife's mind was set on something, it proved of little use trying to get her to change it. Besides, he never could refuse her anything.

Next morning, when Ann, Joan and myself had gone to school, Mother set off for Darlaston.

They would be pleased for her to join them. The manager showed her into the unit, introducing her to the workforce, all of whom suffered some disability.

Fired with enthusiasm Mother made Appleyard's drapery shop the next port of call. She must have a new overall.

'It was a nice little place.' Mother's enthusiasm was still running high when she told us of her visit that evening. 'Everybody was very friendly, med me right welcome they did.'

Monday. The first day of Mother's employment arrived. Her new overall in a brown paper carrier bag along with a cheese sandwich wrapped in newspaper, her boots blacked and her coat on, Mother was ready.

Father had an agreement with his employer from first joining Newman's Tubes which meant that in return for arriving an hour before the start of the working day, opening the place up and lighting the boilers so that by 'clocking on' time production could

begin straight away, Father was allowed time enough
to slip back home. There he would prepare a plate of
buttered toast and set it beside the fire he always lit
before leaving the house. Then he would ensure Hilda
and Phoebe were up and ready to leave for Springs
and Pressings, that us younger ones also had things
for school – shoes polished the night before set beside
gas-mask box, petticoats, vests and knickers warming
on the waist-high fire guard – before returning to
work.

This morning, wife as well as daughters would
leave for the factory.

'Nanny'll be round at quarter to eight,' Mother
said, referring to the neighbour living next door.
'Her'll see the kids gets off to school on time so
you've no need to worry on that.'

'I'll be watchin' for 'em goin' past, same as always.'
It was Father's habit to stand where the huge bay
doors of the works opened onto Holyhead Road so he
could give us a wave as we walked past on our way to
school.

Once Hilda and Phoebe had gone, Mother glanced
at the clock. Five past seven. Time to go, it wouldn't
do to be late the first morning. Taking up her carrier
bag, she left the house. Seven minutes past seven and
she had returned!

In order to provide farmers with a longer period of
daylight the government had adopted 'double sum-

mertime' which meant clocks were put back two hours. This, in combination with the complete absence of street lighting due to bombing raids, had the Lane in pitch darkness.

'George.' Mother's voice had lost a little of its confidence. 'You'll 'ave to come with me, just for the first time.'

He could have told her this would happen, she had not taken into consideration the fact that the streets would be utterly dark and that she'd be walking alone. Diplomatically hiding the smile he knew must not show on his lips he simply nodded when she went on, 'I'll be finishing at six, you'll 'ave to tek time off to fetch me back.'

Tuesday. The second day of Mother's employment.

Routine went as on the previous morning. Nanny Harris would see the kids off to school, there was nothing to worry about.

Agreeing, Father turned to bank the fire before returning to work.

Seven minutes past seven. She had not returned. Ten minutes past seven, still she had not returned. The streets were every bit as dark as they had been the day before, but she must have got over her nerves.

Mother arrived at precisely the moment of that thought.

'You . . . you'll 'ave to come with me . . .'

'What's 'appened? 'As anybody said anything? 'As anybody touched you?'

Anger flaring bright as the fear shining in his wife's eyes Father seized the iron poker.

'No.' Mother shook her head. 'Ain't nobody said nuthin'.'

'So what's the matter?'

'It . . . it's a dog.' Her voice trembled. 'It barked . . . you'll 'ave to come with me!'

Employment beyond the home? For Mother it did not reach a third day.

17

High Days and Holidays

The last fifty years of life saw no holiday for George and none for Annie and her children, unless you counted the year of the trip to Worcester for the annual hop picking.

Some local authorities allowed school children an extra two weeks of holiday, enabling them to accompany their parents to the hop fields, but children living in Staffordshire and attending a school in that county were not given extra holidays and no permission to go hopping was granted. But that did not stop what was an annual exodus, Mother and three of her children a part of it.

The beginning of September was the start of a new school year; it also heralded the start of the hop-picking season. There was no real competition between the two: the latter, with its promise of a break from routine and a little extra for the housekeeping, won hands down. It was also the holiday I remember most clearly.

Sunday was the chosen day for travelling and

boxes and trunks were heaved out of doors ready to be loaded into the 'chara'. It was so exciting to see this coach come down the Lane and the holiday began the moment everyone was aboard and the wheels started to turn. Mothers sang the hits of the day, 'There'll be Bluebirds over the White Cliffs of Dover . . .', 'Run Rabbit Run' and so on until they were hoarse; but in retrospect I think this was to hide the worry they had for husbands and older children left behind to work in the munitions factories; going to Worcester to pick hops didn't mean Hitler and his bombers were also taking that break. Their routine of day and night air raids still continued, and the worry of what might await them on the return home was never truly absent from older people's minds. But for us youngsters the war and its miseries were for that short time forgotten. Even now, sixty years on, I vividly remember the condition of those holiday 'apartments'.

Housed in a cow shed, the walls of which still bore the trace and stench of animals only recently ejected, eight families – four on each side – slept on loose straw, one family sharing a bed partitioned from the next by sacking slung over a line tied to the barn rafters. Water for washing and cooking was obtained via a hand-primed pump, and it was the children's job to fetch this from the farmyard some way off. Cooking could not take place in the barn because of the risk of fire, so much straw bedding being a hazard, so this was done gypsy fashion over an open fire in the yard, or if the weather was wet in a large empty shed.

Bathing was difficult – sharing living space with so many other people meant privacy was almost non-existent. This wasn't so bad for young children: an enamel bowl perched on a stool served the purpose of a bath, but for teenagers and their mothers, embarrassment was lessened by others of the family grouping round the bowl and holding towels for curtains.

But even this inconvenience was outdone by the lavatories. These were no more than a wooden bucket placed in a hole dug into the ground. It was used by the whole community and when it was full, it was picked up by some farm workers, emptied and placed in a fresh hole for the cycle to begin over again.

Mother and several others were dismayed by these conditions and wished to return home, but without money for train fare and the 'chara' not due to return for a month, they were stuck. The one light on Mother's horizon was the visit Father would make on the following Saturday. He would take the Midland Red bus from Wednesbury High Bullen down to Worcester.

Making the best of things was the only option until then. Each day at seven in the morning, washed, dressed and breakfasted, Mother, Ann, myself and

Joan – so young she was placed in the crib, the long canvas-sided container into which the hops were stripped from thirty-foot bines as the trailing growths were called – would be in the field, there to stay until five or six in the evening.

At long last Saturday came, but Father did not. It could only have been pressure of work that kept him from making the journey so Mother was once more forced to accept matters.

The following day I was feeling unwell. Despite the long hours out in the fresh countryside air, I found the stench of that barn where we slept overpowering to say the least, despite copious disinfectant and scrubbing of the floor space between the straw beds. Whether or not it was this that caused my sickness I only know that over the hours I gradually felt worse until eventually the doctor had to be called. His diagnosis was yellow jaundice and I was not to be moved.

I could not be taken from the bed, but no work meant no money and that equalled no food. There was no alternative. Mother must continue with the hop picking while I remain alone in the barn, Ann running back every half hour to make sure I was all right.

That week was interminable. The only relief came when the evening chores were finished and an old wind-up gramophone – brought in the luggage of one of the other families – was placed on the 'bath' stool, the same few records crackling their songs over and again through the brass horn. One of these I learned from listening to that wheezing recording and sang it often to my own daughters when they were small.

'I don't want to play in your yard,
You don't love me any more,
You'll be sorry when you see me
Swinging on my garden door . . .'

The voice would sing and I would try singing with it.

'You shan't climb my apple tree,
I don't want to play in your yard
If you're not good to me.'

Maybe the years have blurred the exact words but I still get pleasure singing my hop-yard song.

Father, however, sang a very different song when he arrived the second Saturday after our leaving home, and his ditty held no trace of pleasure. Taking one look at his babby lying on that bed of straw, my skin, even the whites of my eyes a sallow yellow, he told Mother to pack her things.

A tussle with the farmer followed for he declared he could pay no one what was owed until the picking season was over. Eventually he agreed to exchange the metal tokens recording the amount already due for cash. One of the women sharing the barn agreed to see Mother's box put on the coach when it returned to fetch them back. Then, disregarding the

Library, Wednesbury

The Bandstand, Wednesbury Park

Tube Workers

Newmans Tubery

Mother Outside the Anderson Shelter

Hop Picking

Cookery Lesson, Holyhead Road School

St James School Teachers [with thanks to
Alice Cartwright and Gladys Ward for their
help identifying staff]

Miss Harris, the headmistress
[with thanks to Mrs Dorothy Rose]

VE Day Celebrations, Britannia wins the day

VE Day Celebrations, 'Eagles Shop', Paul Street, Wednesbury

Ralph, aged eighteen

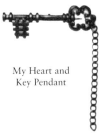

My Heart and
Key Pendant

Me, one month short of my
fifteenth birthday

Hilda

Ann

Me

Joan

Phoebe

George's Lasses

Mom and Dad, 1957

doctor's advice, Father picked me up and carried me home, followed by the rest of the family.

There were no more hop-picking holidays.

High days, though few and far between enough before the advent of war, now became even fewer. Father would visit his local – though this too became less frequent as beer became more and more scarce – but as the air raids grew heavier Mother stopped leaving the house in the evenings. With one exception. Some relative in Wolverhampton had a son being married before being sent abroad. An invitation arrived and it was agreed Mother and Father would attend the evening 'do', returning home around nine. Hilda and Phoebe were deemed old enough to babysit the rest of us for the two hours or so Mother and Father would be away.

That was fine. We played hunt the thimble and when that palled we each demonstrated the song and dance skills learned at the Clapperettes. Then, at around eight-thirty, Hilda announced bed time for Ann, Joan and me. It was during our vociferous refusals that the sirens sounded the alarm.

We knew we should go to the shelter in the garden, but even with candles to light it and Father there to guard against spiders and toads, the shelter was an eerie place and the prospect of going there was even less acceptable than going to bed had been. Hearing

the well-known shout of 'Put that light out', and
thinking maybe there was a hole in the curtains where
a chink might be showing, Hilda had no option but to
switch off the electricity. Huddled together around
the fireplace, we listened to the drone of planes, the
thud of bombs falling in the distance, the bump,
bump of 'pom pom' guns, firing from their anti-
aircraft positions, the shouts and whistles of air-raid
wardens. Mother and Father would be home about
nine; we had not long to wait.

Ten o' clock came, but no parents. What if Mr
Siveter the air-raid warden called and ordered us into
the shelter? Whispered thoughts more frightening than
enemy bombs, we sat with hearts thumping. But maybe
there was too much else for Mr Siveter to do for he did
not make his usual call at the house. No one came. Not
even our parents. Too afraid to go to bed, tiredness
bringing Joan and me to tears, we all lay together on the
hearth like a line of little tin soldiers, Hilda at one end,
Phoebe at the other, and all the time the sounds of war.

Where was Mother? Where was Father? Why
didn't they come? Hilda was patient with her weeping
younger sisters but her quiet assurance that 'Mom
and Dad will be here in a minute' wore a ragged edge.
Usually bossy, seeing her extra few years as licence to
order the rest of us around, tonight she forgot to be
dictatorial, taking turns with Phoebe to tell stories or
recite a poem.

Then Joan needed a wee. Which was worse, letting her sister wet her knickers or taking her outside to the lavatory? While Hilda pondered the dilemma, I decided I also needed the 'lav'; at this Ann joined in. Three of us all needing to spend a penny – there would be the devil to pay if Mother found three sets of wet knickers.

It needed a lot of courage. Who knew what waited in the darkness beyond the kitchen door? There was no electric light in the toilet, nor could it have been switched on if there had been; a candle then? But that too was out of the question, its glow would be seen from the street. So it was face the darkness.

Declaring she wasn't going to remain in the house alone, Phoebe joined the scared little troupe clinging to Hilda as she led the way. The toilet of Number 51 Dangerfield Lane, like each of its neighbours, was joined to the kitchen. Opposite was the coalhouse, the space between the two forming a small covered entrance from the garden path. Hilda at the front, none of us four wanting to be last, we jammed into the cramped two-yard-wide square. Beyond the garden wall a street lamp shone its relieving light illuminating our lavatory, so that normally we felt no loss from its possessing no light of its own. But these were not normal times, the streetlamps were unlit and the heavy blackness of a sky crisscrossed with silver lances of searchlights only added depth to the shadows and tingles to our spines.

Knickers left about the ankles, one sister hurried from the toilet while another dashed in. We would definitely have taken gold in any Olympic event that night as, nature attended to, we ran back into the living room.

The tin clock with its large bell on top showed its black fingers in firelight. Almost eleven o' clock. Something terrible must have happened to Mother and Father, they would never leave us alone like this were they able to come home. It must have been a bomb . . . Were they lying injured somewhere? Were they dead?

Fear mounting upon fear, tears flowing afresh, Hilda tried to soothe us. She lit a candle and placed it beneath the table so the folds of the tablecloth might shield the pale glow from the window, then she settled us down again on the hearth and there we lay, five young girls with arms wrapped about one another while hell raged outside.

There were no stories now, no poetry, just the flickering of a candle and the catch of frightened breath as the thuds and whines of falling bombs seemed to come ever nearer; then, with an ear-shattering explosion, one found its target. The ground beneath us shook, the house walls seemed to tremble then shouts and whistles from the street told us the bomb had struck waste ground behind a factory situated at the Darlaston end of the Lane. We were so petrified the screams wouldn't leave our throats. Then, miraculously, Father was there. Taking the two youngest in his arms, the other three following close, he shepherded us into the garden shelter.

But where was Mother? Why wasn't she with him? His youngest daughters still held close on either knee, words interrupted by the scream of missiles, he explained. The warning siren had sounded some time before nine, followed very quickly by the first drones of approaching planes. Dreading a heavy raid and knowing Mother's crippled leg would keep her from running from where the tram would drop them at the Bull Stake, Father spent minutes convincing her it would be best if he came home alone. Leaving her to take shelter with the other guests assembled at the wedding celebration, he sprinted for the tram stop. It was several more minutes, in which the skies became white with searchlights, before a conductor returning from his shift at the tram depot informed Father that all vehicles were withdrawn from service for the duration of the raid, the danger of their lights being seen by bombers flying overhead too great a risk.

But his kids were alone in the house and like to be frightened out of their wits. Not pausing to think would he, could he run so far, Father set off. Ignoring police and air-raid wardens telling him to get off the streets, to take cover in one of the shelters, he ran, walking only when breath threatened to desert him but never once stopping until the seven miles were covered and he was home.

I said holidays and highlights were few and far between. After that night they ceased completely, Mother refusing to be parted from her babbies.

18

Leisure and Pleasure

Today leisure and pleasure are liberally on offer and thankfully can be enjoyed by many, but for my parents they were few and far between. Yet now and then the humdrum routine was alleviated, if only for an hour or so.

One such occasion came when Mother, having heard over and again of the marvellous film showing at the Olympia in Darlaston, made up her mind to go to see it and to take me with her.

Olympia! The name conveys a sense of grandeur, of something elegant and beautiful. In truth it was the local flea pit. A dowdy run-down exterior housed hard uncushioned seats and a bare wood floor quite unlike the more recently built Regal, which boasted an upper circle, red upholstered seats and carpeted floors. But the Regal was not showing the film Mother wanted to see.

The weather was overcast as we walked to Darlaston Green, it would most likely be raining by the time the film was over, but at nine years old, with the grand prospect of going to the pictures dancing a tango in my mind, the state of the weather was not of the least importance.

A queue had already formed along the narrow pavement bordering the 'Limp'; maybe we wouldn't get a seat. This possibility plagued my mind as I stared hypnotised at the posters pasted onto the brickwork of the tired-looking cinema.

A beautiful woman and a dark-haired man gazed implacably beneath a banner headline . . . 'Clark Gable and Vivienne Leigh in . . . Gone With The Wind.'

The evening kept to the promise of delight, the stifled sobs of women and the quiet coughs of men confirming their enjoyment. Mother often cried when something made her happy and tonight was no exception.

From time to time, in the moments of quiet between battle scenes, it seemed a noise from somewhere in the building penetrated the darkened auditorium but, entranced by the suffering of the American South, and the stubborn infatuation and desire of Scarlett O'Hara for another woman's husband, no member of the audience gave mind to anything apart from the scenes flitting across that screen . . . until a resounding roar echoed above the voices of actors and the sound of background music.

Then the film disappeared.

This had the picture house in an immediate uproar.

Only half of the film had been shown! Why had it been taken off? A few minutes later the reason was flashed onto the screen.

'Ladies and gentlemen. The management regrets to announce that due to storm damage outside the showing of tonight's film will not continue. Refunds will be made at the box office.'

Not continue! Refunds! The entire audience erupted, feet sounding a tattoo of displeasure, shouts demanded the film go on.

Perhaps it was the vehemence of those demands that made the manager decide to allow the film to run through to completion. Certainly Mother and I were two of an audience that made no attempt to leave until it was over.

It was only when we emerged outside into the street the reason for the brief interruption became obvious. Part of the roof of the building was missing.

Gone with the wind indeed!

It could be said war steals childhood. Certainly for the children of the Second World War it stole much of what makes childhood memorable.

Those years of conflict meant shortages of almost everything and luxuries such as chocolates and sweets were in short supply and bananas and other fruits grown abroad disappeared altogether, at least for the children of Dangerfield Lane.

War also robbed us of the wonderful excitement of
the circus, of the visits of Pat Collins Fair, which
turned a patch of bare ground along Catherine's
Cross into a fairyland of brilliant lights. The music
of a Calliope, a huge steam-operated organ complete
with garishly painted wooden figures, vied with steam
whistles in a cacophony of music that blared out over
roll-a-penny stalls and rides decked in colourful
lights, the volume of sound almost drowning the calls
of barkers advertising the wonders, delights and
terrors waiting to be seen 'for only thruppence'.

Where had it all gone? And why could Halloween
no longer be celebrated with lanterns and candle jars
in the street? Why was November Fifth no longer
marked by fireworks while a stuffed replica of Guy
Fawkes met its end in the flames of a huge bonfire?
Christmas, too, was diminished. A tree made from a
broom stave and branches of privet wrapped around
in newspaper, then draped with tinsel dulled from use
year upon year might not have been *so* disappointing,
but decked in candles and fairy lights which could not
be lit! The magic was gone.

With this in mind it takes little imagination to
picture the pleasure I felt when one afternoon I came
home from school and Mother handed me one shilling and sixpence, telling me I could go to the pictures
along with Joan.

This time the cinema was the Picture Drome.

Heady with excitement at this unlooked-for treat, Joan and I were off up the Lane, taking the short cut over the clay knobs, high mounds of pit waste from the no longer existent Lodge Holes Colliery, which led directly onto Pinfold Street. A few minutes later and we reached the cinema, which was located further into Darlaston town at Victoria Crescent.

The auditorium was every bit as run down as that of the Olympia, but I breathed pure joy when the house lights lowered and first house showing began. Forthcoming attractions, trailers of films to be shown the following week, adverts for various businesses – all added to the pleasure, as did the fine droplets of moisture twinkling like minute silver stars in the stream of light coming from the projection box. With them came a most agreeable scent.

Seduced by the pleasing aroma I took my attention from the screen to watch the usherette come along the aisle. Drawing almost level with the row of seats in which Joan and I were seated she lifted the stirrup pump high into the air. Determined to be caught in the issuing cloud of perfume, I craned towards the scintillating shower. It was years before I learned the liquid sprayed several times during every performance shown in that cinema was not the perfume I thought, but disinfectant used against fleas!

But that evening it enhanced an enjoyment nothing could spoil. Or so I thought!

Then the 'B' film, shorter in duration than the 'big picture', began. I cannot recall the title but I well remember the lead character. Andy Clyde was playing a comic role. Roars of laughter followed each antic until one which had him supposedly forced head first between the large wooden rollers of a mangle, a flat cardboard cut-out of him emerging on the other side. The laughter this produced was joined by a terrified scream from Joan. No amount of comforting, of explaining the man was simply pretending to be put through the mangle, had any effect on Joan; she was frightened and wailed for her mom.

There was nothing for it. Shining her torch along the seats, the usherette who minutes before had sprayed that delightful perfume was now demanding we leave the cinema.

'Never mind, luv.' She smiled kindly as I walked dejectedly out to the drab foyer, a crying younger sister clinging desperately to my hand. 'You tek the little 'un 'ome then you can come back, I'll tell the box office you don't 'ave to pay again.'

Joan refused to return via the clay knobs, which would cut the time taken to reach home by more than half; the wicked men who had put another man through the mangle might be there waiting to do the same to her. This was Joan's train of thought and nothing was going to derail it. The longer route took even more time because of Joan's insistent clinging that hampered every step. Once there, we found Mother had gone to visit Aunt Phoebe, Father was on fire-watching duty and Ann, the only occupant, refused to be saddled with a still almost hysterical Joan.

Aunt Phoebe's house in Margaret Road was a couple of minutes' fast run from ours in the Lane, but Joan's legs refused to run. But at last, at long last, I had helped Mother get my distressed sister home and I was once more seated in that darkened auditorium.

My pleasure was short-lived. Some fifteen minutes later the entire programme of films ended. The next showing, the second house, would not begin until a quarter to eight. Staying until then was not even contemplated. One thing Mother would not stand for was to have either of her younger daughters walk home alone in the dark.

So much for my treat!

Andy Clyde has not been forgotten; even now, so long after that visit to the 'Drome', mention of his being put through the mangle brings a shudder to Joan's spine.

19

Reconciliation?

Three years into the war and after two years of earning her living in Springs and Pressings factory at Darlaston Green, Hilda longed for the adventure of a holiday away from home. Talking it over with her friend Vera Preece they reckoned they had both saved enough from the money they were allowed to keep from their weekly wage to pay for a few days at the seaside. All they really needed now was parental permission.

Times were dangerous with the almost nightly visits of Hitler's air forces but Mother and Father agreed: if their daughter could work during that threat then she deserved to play through a little of it. So at sixteen years old, Hilda was ready for her first real holiday.

This was almost over before it began. As they stood on the platform of Walsall railway station the whistle of the approaching train caused the two girls to pick up their cases only to be knocked off their feet by other travellers surging forward in the press to find a seat. Caught in the rush, Hilda was sent flying over the edge of the platform and onto the line. Just yards away, the train steamed towards the figure now sprawled in its path and, as if turned to stone, no other person moved. Except for Ann who had gone to see the two of them off. Staring first at the belching black monster, then at the sister it was threatening to kill, she dropped flat onto her stomach and literally hauled Hilda by her coat to the safety of the platform.

But the drama didn't spoil the excitement of a holiday. Pressing Ann to say nothing of this harrowing incident, Hilda and Vera waved her from the train now heading to Blackpool.

When they saw their room in the boarding house they had booked, the sixteen-year-olds looked in amazement at the three double beds it held. A bed each! This was a luxury they had never known before! As it transpired they were not to know it now either. Some half an hour after setting their cases on their chosen bed, Hilda and Vera were joined by four more young women. The holidaymakers would each have to share with a friend.

The next day after breakfast Hilda set about the one mission Father had requested she accomplish. His last words before she had left the house had been, 'Go see your grandmother.'

The address where Florence lived had long been known to Father via his 'sisters' Mary and Maud, who still lived in Wednesbury. Because she wanted some recognition from the woman who had abandoned him, our mother had sent Florence a Christmas card for several years after she and Father married. All were ignored. But hope dies hard and Hilda's visit to Blackpool was no doubt seen by Father as offering the possibility of a reconciliation: perhaps seeing her granddaughter might do what Christmas cards had not.

Going to go visit someone she had never met, a mother who had turned her back on a three-month-old boy, a woman who had made no attempt to contact him, who made no acknowledgement of the Christmas cards Mother sent every year, who, it seemed obvious, had no desire to know Father, did not sit well with Hilda. But neither did the alternative, the disappointment she knew Father would feel should she not make the visit. So Hilda and Vera made their way to the house in Peter Street.

A woman much taller than Hilda's five foot three, and fairly heavily built, answered the door. Her dark brown hair was neatly curled and her eyes as vividly blue as Father's, but her face lost a little of its colour when Hilda said quietly, 'My name is Hilda Astbury, I live in Wednesbury.'

The girls were conducted into the kitchen but not invited to sit down. They refused the 'welcoming' drink of a spoonful of powdered milk stirred into a glass of cold water.

Florence said there were a large number of guests presently boarding at the house and consequently she was very busy, however they must have a drink on her.

They had been as good as told to leave! The grandmother Hilda had never met did not wish to know her now.

Glancing dismissively at the half crown Florence had placed upon the table, Hilda was at her haughty best.

'No.'

She looked coldly at the woman who was her father's mother.

'You must have a drink on me.'

Taking a pound note from her bag, she placed it beside the half crown, then, without another word, walked out of the kitchen and away from Peter Street.

The point had been made. Florence had never offered money and now she had been shown it was not welcome; though with Father working thirteen, sometimes more hours a day, often six days a week for less than six pounds, it can be understood just how much monetary value a pound held. But that was nothing compared to the value of Hilda's satisfaction in showing just how little her grandmother's charity was needed.

The reception shown Hilda should have proved the final attempt at reunion between mother and son but, ever optimistic, Father made the same request again some years later when Ann and her friend Ivy Bladen also went to holiday at Blackpool.

Once again the visit to the boarding house in Peter Street was made. This time a less robustly built woman, looking to be in her mid-thirties, sat on the short flight of steps, two young children beside her.

'My father asked me to call.'

Ann glanced up at the older woman who had come to stand at the head of the steps. Though no introduction was made the facial resemblance between Florence and the younger woman was such as to lead Ann to assume they were mother and daughter.

'My name is Ann Astbury, my father's name is George Henry.'

A tightening of the mouth together with the same slight drain of colour intimating her recognition, the woman invited Ann and Ivy to take a seat . . . on the steps.

No introductions, no enquiries as to a long-abandoned son – Florence offered no more than a biscuit. Ann refused as her sister had refused a glass of powdered milk, but she, canny lass, left no pound note to mark her visit.

Each of George's five daughters and also his wife

visited Blackpool many times but none went again to the house in Peter Street, nor did George make the journey himself; somehow he could not find the courage to seek out the mother who regardless of her treatment of him was never gone completely from his heart.

But there was no reunion, no reconciliation.

In his sixty-fourth year George died without having once seen or spoken to the woman who had given him birth.

20

Not Quite Shakespeare!

Transferring into Senior School was an automatic process. At eleven years of age came the change from the primary level to that of Senior, later to become known as Secondary Modern and later still to undergo several more changes of description to comply with the whims of government.

In many schools this transfer meant pupils relocating to other sections of the building, as it did with girls attending St James' Church of England School.

Moving to the upper rooms they now became students of St James' Church of England School for Girls, but at eleven the boys were moved to St Bartholomew's situated near the centre of town. This exchange of boys for girls and vice versa continued until both schools finally closed.

Transferring into the Seniors wrought a change in my attitude to school. Suddenly I was interested in what was taught and lessons became enjoyable – all, that is, except physical education. PE was top of my list of things to avoid. Once again my talent for deception came into play.

Discipline, though fair, was strict and the rule of not talking in class unless in answer to a teacher's question was rigidly observed. There lay my avenue of escape, and I was to run down it regularly.

St James' school was not blessed with facilities such as changing rooms, nor did its pupils possess a PE kit. Dresses and petticoats were removed in the classroom and the lesson, consisting of marking time on the spot, bending to touch the toes or vaulting over the back of a partner, took place in the hall. Jigging about in vest and knickers was not for me, especially not as I developed breasts . . . with no bra (lack of money again!) to prevent this part of my generous anatomy jiggling. Embarrassment demanded I find a way of avoiding this lesson altogether.

I found it quite easily.

Waiting one morning for the dreaded words 'Clothes off, girls', I deliberately turned to whisper to the girl next to me. This had the desired effect. From her desk positioned on a raised platform, Mrs Hadley stared. This offence could not go unpunished.

Pointing an accusing finger she declared in tones unmistakably showing her displeasure, 'Margaret Astbury . . . you will not do PE this morning, you will write me a composition instead!'

Not only had my strategy worked, it had brought an added bonus!

Reading a book or writing a story had been favourite pastimes of mine since as far back as I could remember, so instead of punishing my insubordination, Mrs Hadley had inadvertently rewarded it. The ruse followed through most of my years in the Senior department, and in all honesty I cannot say I feel regret. Did Mrs Hadley and my subsequent teachers not notice the game I was playing? Of course they did; but they knew also of my passion for reading and especially for creative writing. Turning a blind eye to my repeated attempts to miss out on PE was, I truly believe, their way of encouraging that.

Years after staging that first Cinderella was to come a second attempt at theatre production, though this would not be staged in the garden of 51 Dangerfield Lane, nor would it have an audience watching from bedroom windows.

1945 was the centenary year of St James' School. To mark this a special mass would be celebrated. Singing of the Creed would be followed by a prayer to be sung in Latin. Latin! Half the kids had difficulty learning the words in English. Their version of the Lord's prayer was 'Our Father who art in heaven, 'Arold be thy name . . .' Hymns, too, had an entirely different wording, the rendering of

'Firmly I believe and truly' coming out as 'firmly I believe in Julie'. As for me, I simply learned the newly introduced Ave Maria parrot fashion, singing it over and over at home to Mother's everlasting pride. So seriously did I take the learning, so devotedly did I attend Sunday morning and afternoon church service, she became convinced I would take the veil and become a nun.

The celebration planned by Father Philip Husbands was not the only one. Miss Harris, the then Head of the Senior Girls School, determined they also would mark the occasion. The fact we had received no tuition in the writing of a theatrical script proved no obstacle to Miss Harris.

'This morning you will write a play – you may choose the theme for yourself.'

Thank you, Miss Harris!

No further guidance deemed necessary she proceeded to mark the morning's arithmetic work. But the shock did not end there. Plays duly written were collected and next day came the announcement. Two of them had been selected for production; one written by Pamela Harris (no relation to the Headmistress!) the other, by Margaret Astbury.

I can't remember the one written by Pamela Harris – forgive me, Pam, we will laugh over a cup of tea – but the one written by me was the usual fantasy of a dying parent whose only hope lay in the finding of a magical blue flower, a petal of which laid on the lips gave instant recovery.

The trials, tribulations and setbacks that provided the body of the play would not have caused Steven Spielberg to lose sleep, nor was the finale with its happy ending quite in league with today's sagas and romantic fiction, but it gave me a few headaches.

The authors, it was proclaimed by Miss Harris, would be solely responsible for casting – not a mammoth problem considering each author was a member of an eager peer group. If only that had proved to be the end of it, but no! In addition to casting, creating costumes, scripts, in effect everything, including auditioning every girl in school hopeful of a part, the productions would be performed before an audience of visiting church dignitaries.

Admittedly we were allowed time free from lessons in order to rehearse, but it still seemed a mammoth task for a fourteen-year-old to take on alone.

We raided the dressing-up box kept below a set of stairs in Mrs Hadley's classroom and enlisted help from Mother and somehow Miss Harris' edict was fulfilled. Then at a dress rehearsal, I found Pamela's production included a song. A song! Why hadn't I thought of that? On the way home cousin Mary, who was playing the helpful guardian witch, declared it was much too late to insert a song with only twenty-four hours to go before the big day. But 'too late' were words I wouldn't hear. A song was included in Pamela's production, so a song would be included in mine! Luckily a part of our music lesson – given via the school wireless – had been the words and music of Brahms Cradle Song, and more luckily still, it fitted the final scene of the play perfectly.

Came the great day. Mother had received a special invitation requesting her to be present. She had attended this school herself and now she was to see one of her own children act in a play there. She sat on one of some dozen or so reserved chairs in the front. She looked so small among the clergy, dressed some in robes of plain black or in robes touched with scarlet. Here was a sight we children had not seen before, so found it a little unnerving; but Mother's nervousness was lost beneath a glow of pride. Her daughter had sung a prayer in Latin, her daughter's play had been chosen to mark the day of the school's centenary – yes she was proud!

Many times since that day I have hummed or sung the Latin words drummed so relentlessly into my brain; words sung once for a church service and no more after that. But just what had I sung? There had been no explanation, no translation, and none of us had the courage to ask. It was just one more case of do as you are told and don't ask questions.

As I did not ask it came as something of a surprise to learn, years later, that Ave Maria meant Hail Mary and my parrot-fashion song was the prayer we said each morning during religious assembly.

Along with its absence of air-raid shelters and changing rooms, St James' School lacked facilities for the teaching of cookery and the subject then termed 'housewifery'. But it was part of the curriculum and had to be included.

But how?

The solution was the same as it had been with the question of air-raid shelters: we would share with another school.

In the event of an air attack the whole school had travelled some quarter of a mile along the busy Holyhead Road in order to take cover in the shelters erected alongside the school of that same name; now as Senior girls we would travel twice the distance in the opposite direction in order to be given weekly instruction on how to make a meal, how to wash an article of clothing or how to scrub a floor. All of which we had long ago been taught by our mothers.

Ingredients for the dish of the week could not always be come by, for food rationing was hard and strict. The same applied to soap needed for laundry or the scrubbing of the floor; it, too, was in short supply. This obstacle was overcome for us by Father's 'borrowing' of a small, thin tablet of hard brown soap used in the factory.

But whatever you might or might not have had in the way of ingredients, you absolutely had to have 'cookery uniform'.

Consisting of cap and apron, this was made by each girl during needlework, every handmade stitch having to conform to a set length and size. If it did not, then the whole lot had to be taken out and you started all over again.

Washed and boiled, rinsed in Rickett's Blue – a solution which increased the level of whiteness – then starched so it almost stood up on its own, cap and apron were produced and inspected for any slight mark or offending crease before we set out, unaccompanied by any member of staff, for the Lower High Street Board School. Any girl whose uniform did not pass muster found herself left behind to scrub and clean the classroom cupboard.

Not much changes. Cap and apron were of identical design for girls of St James' School as those of the girls attending Holyhead Road, that establishment once again offering use of room and facilities on the odd occasions when the Board School could not.

Almost as dire as not having brought the required cap and apron was the lack of any garment to launder. Arriving in the domestic science room I found I had forgotten to bring the artificial silk petticoat loaned by Lizzie Noon. It was too late for me to be left behind to scrub cupboards! But the teacher in charge of the class had another idea. I could wash a garment of hers.

She handed it to me as I stood at the sink and could not help but see the look of disgust which flashed across my face. The garment was a pair of knickers, and they were stained with blood.

I knew what periods were. I also knew they sometimes arrived unexpectedly and as a result knickers became unavoidably soiled. But I had never been made to wash any pair myself, Mother always took care of that.

Having to rub that blood-soaked cloth between my fingers, dipping my hands again and again into water turned red, made my insides cringe. I wanted nothing so much as to walk away and leave the woman to wash her own soiled underwear.

Why could she not have sent me back to St James'? Wasn't that the usual procedure with girls who turned up minus any article or ingredient for the afternoon's instruction?

I looked again at the knickers. Scrubbing a classroom cupboard would have been infinitely preferable to washing these.

'You may scrub the gusset.' The teacher stood at my elbow. 'But carefully, girl, you are not scrubbing a floor!'

How I wished I was!

At last the knickers were deemed suitably prepared

for the boiler. Holding them with pincer-shaped laundry tongs, I plunged them into the bubbling soapy water. *Now* I could scrub out the pantry.

On hands and knees. I thought of what Mother would say should she know of the tasks I had been given. 'Serves you right for being careless.' I also remembered the words she was heard to murmur when things had not gone right for her: 'Life be a penny dip, you don't always get the prize you would have.'

How true! I had certainly drawn the booby prize that day. It taught me a hard lesson but a useful one. From that day on, I checked I had everything needed for those afternoons of domestic science.

21

Sisters, Sisters

'Never were there such devoted sisters.' Those are the words of a popular song and though in the main they ring true for the daughters of Annie and George, devotion is not always so elastic it does not threaten to break.

Staunch in support of each other beyond the home, each of us ready to floor the boy or girl who dared raise a hand to any one of us, we weren't always willing to turn a blind eye if one sister annoyed another.

Like any family we had our differences and sometimes these led to a scrap, Hilda and Phoebe being no exception.

Phoebe was the most lovable rogue; all through life she had charisma, a charm Father declared 'would fetch the ducks off the water'. While at school she was regularly involved in fights, leaving Hilda to face the music when teachers demanded to know the whys and wherefores. Then there were times the unfortunate Hilda was given the task of explaining to our irate

mother those situations where, having gone out together, one daughter returned home at the specified
time while the other did not.

Given errands to do one evening after school they
clattered to the shops together, Hilda going to Butler's
grocer shop, Phoebe to the butcher.

Several women, all of whom seemed more interested in gossiping with the grocer and with
other customers than in being served themselves,
meant it was some time before Hilda was attended
to.

No sooner had she emerged than a crumpled
package was thrust at her and Phoebe was off at
the gallop, calling she had to go to the library.

Her warning about being late home falling on
empty air Hilda placed the package in the basket
alongside the rest of the shopping. One day Phoebe
was going to get herself into real trouble!

Trouble did not find Phoebe that afternoon but it
did find Hilda.

What was this? Mother's frown was ominous when
the crumpled package was opened. Gone were the
sausages she was expecting, the sausages she had sent
Phoebe to the butcher's to buy; in their place a string
of empty skins. Phoebe had been up to her old trick of
squeezing the sausage meat out of the skin and eating
it. It's a habit that followed her into adult life, and I
must admit it was one I myself was also guilty of. In

the days I write about, sausage meat was meat, not the soya-laden product of today.

The library! Instantly Hilda recognised the reason behind Phoebe running off. She had eaten the sausage meat leaving her sister to face the music. She ought to have known! Listening to Mother's promised reward of a 'smacked arse for that little bugger when 'er comes in', Hilda had her own reward in mind. Phoebe would pay for her little prank.

'I did have to go to the library!'

Walking back from school next day Phoebe defended her action, but Hilda was having none of it.

'You never go to the library, you've got no interest in reading, even if you are told to find information on a subject for the next day's lessons you never do it yourself, you depend on me reading it for you and then telling you what you need to know. Well, I'm not doing it again if you leave me to explain empty sausage skins!'

'I didn't know they were empty.' Eyes wide and innocent as they had been when called to book by Mother, Phoebe persisted in the lie which had spared her bottom from the proposed smacking.

'Of course you did, you liar, the butcher isn't daft enough to sell you empty skins!'

Miffed at being left to carry the can while, as always, her sister got away scot-free, Hilda still smarted.

'. . . and you didn't go to no library neither, it's my bet you went walking the railway bridge or jumping the brook.'

Keeping a wary distance, Phoebe grinned impishly. 'Well your bet be wrong.'

'You *didn't* go to the library!'

'Never said I did. I were climbing the rock by the Donkey Bridge, and I'm gonna climb it again now.'

Legs flashing like a young colt's she darted away.

They had both been specifically warned not to play there and definitely not to climb the large boulder formed from the tipping of slag – waste from the furnaces of Monway and Old Park steel foundries – and dumped on ground which years before had been a cornfield. This huge lump of solidified dross was a favourite with children. Daring each other to climb to the top then jump off, saying any who refused was a cissy, they made it a regular stopping-off place between school and home.

She knew she should not follow, but as Hilda watched the fast-receding figure, she couldn't help wanting just a couple of jumps!

The game was in full swing by the time she got there and the laughter, the jostling and sheer exhilaration of it chased away her ill humour. Hilda was soon in the thick of things.

One after another they climbed, lads imitating

Tarzan's famous cry as they leaped, others dancing up and down on the summit while awaiting their turn to jump, landing sprawling or lying prostrate in a pretence of being injured only to spring up and once more ascend the rock.

Jimmy Skinner, a lad in the same class as Hilda, called to his friends to wait while he climbed alone. What did he have in mind? Standing a little way off they watched him haul himself to the summit, perform several acrobatic leaps and, pretending a dive into water, he launched himself off.

Shouts applauded this new stunt and laughter accompanied the 'swimmer' doing breast stroke on the ground. But suddenly the exuberance halted, cheers strangled in shocked throats. The mass of rock which afforded them so much fun had collapsed, trapping the boy and killing him instantly.

Not realising what had happened, no one spoke for several moments. Then the fun of the stunt turned to boredom. Skinner's larking about was good for a laugh but it was going on too long, it was holding up the game.

'Get up, Jimmy.'

'C'mon, Jim, stop acting daft.'

Impatiently, several of the lads called out. But the figure on the ground made no answer.

'You'm spoiling the game.'

'We've all seen your Tarzan act.'

'C'mon, it ain't funny any more!' Call as they did, it made no difference, the boy did not move.

'Is he all right?'

'D'you think he's hurt himself?'

Among the girls, questions slipped from mouth to mouth. This was too much. Taller than the rest of them, one lad issued the ultimatum.

'We'm gonna climb up so you best shift now or we jump on you!'

'What's he doing?' Phoebe pulled at Hilda's sleeve. 'Why don't he get up?'

But Hilda didn't answer. She felt the same anxiety beginning to show on several faces. Why didn't Jimmy move? Why didn't he laugh and call out it was all a joke meant to scare them?

'Make him get up!' Annoyed at having her fun interrupted, Phoebe stared challengingly at the tallest lad.

'C'mon.' He nodded to a couple of his friends. 'We'll shift 'im.'

Going to where Jimmy lay, silent and unmoving, the three bent to drag him clear of the landing space, then their faces suddenly lost colour. Their bravado dropped away and they stepped back.

'He's . . . he's bleeding . . . I think he's knocked himself out!'

The game was forgotten. Frightened whispers ran like shadows among the watching group. Jimmy was bleeding! Jimmy was hurt! Why didn't they lift him up?

But they couldn't lift him, the rock was lying partly across his body. Jimmy was trapped.

What to do? Scared faces looked at one another.

What did you do when something was so wrong that you couldn't do anything about it yourself? In Hilda's mind the answer was obvious. You fetched your mother.

Suggesting that Jimmy's parents be fetched brought scared whimpers of 'not me', 'I ain't going', until finally one boy who lived next door to the family said he would do it. With that the group fled in panic.

Knowing that both she and Phoebe would be in trouble for being at the Donkey Bridge and climbing the rock, and in even more trouble if they stayed to see the injured body being moved, Hilda followed suit.

The next day, gathered together for morning school assembly, we heard the news. Jimmy Skinner was dead, killed by that falling rock.

As usual with youngsters, the lesson was quickly forgotten. One hazardous playground was swapped for another. After all, where was the fun if there was no risk?

This was the motto of the time and as today proves only too clearly, times don't change.

Children do, however, grow into teenagers. But

Phoebe saw this as no reason to change her roguish behaviour, which sometimes resulted in her and Hilda fighting like she-cats, rolling around the floor until in exasperation Mother would bring the bout to a halt by dousing them in cold water. An hour later the devoted sisters would trot off together to the local dance held in Wednesbury's St Mary's Church hall or the drill hall used on other nights for training Darlaston Home Guard.

One aspect of Phoebe's behaviour soon developed into a major source of annoyance for Hilda. The borrowing of her clothes. She was careful with the pocket money from her weekly wage, saving the greater part while Phoebe spent hers almost the moment Mother handed it to her.

In these early years of leaving school they would use their priceless clothing coupons buying material they then had made into matching dresses designed between them. But as time went on Hilda's carefully saved pennies became enough to buy dresses from Rose Woolf, the most fashionable store in Wednesbury, from Bishop and Marston of Darlaston and even the grander Beattie's of Wolverhampton and Lewis's of Birmingham. These were teamed with precious satin petticoats and, the new craze, cami-knickers.

But why spend money on things you can have anyway? Better to keep it for visits to the pictures or for indulging in any other of the delights life had to offer. This was Phoebe's philosophy and she embraced it with enthusiasm.

You know what's said about best-laid plans? Phoebe's worked well – for a while!

Her strategy was simple. Arriving home from the factory, she would wash in the bathroom then nip upstairs to change, reappearing already attired in buttoned-up coat. Without coming into the living-room, she would call jauntily, 'Off now, Mom, see you later,' then saunter through the front door and away up the Lane.

Coming and going through the front door of 51 Dangerfield Lane had never been the custom. Weddings and funerals were the only times it was opened without a feeling of nervous apprehension, the rare occasion of a knock on it bringing the house to silence, each one of its occupants mouthing the words, 'Who can it be?' Yet here was Phoebe gaily tripping out through the front door.

Another foible? Since Hilda had married and Phoebe had found new friends, she had developed an assortment of these, one being changing her name to Pat. 'I can't go telling people my name is Phoebe, it's so old fashioned!' This was the explanation Mother got when the postman delivered a letter addressed to Miss 'Pat' Astbury.

So the practice went on, until one evening as she

tripped down the path towards the garden gate Hilda spotted the petticoat peeping below Phoebe's hemline. Any glimpse of underwear being regarded as 'racy' and certainly not to be shown by decent girls, Phoebe was recalled.

Back in the living room the tell-tale sign proved the petticoat to be new, unworn, and belonging to Hilda! The game was up.

Righteous indignation had its owner grasp the hem and snatch down hard. The petticoat dropped about Phoebe's ankles with a soft satin sigh. But that was not enough for Hilda. So many years of covering up her sister's little white lies, of explaining her often madcap behaviour, made Hilda suspicious; just what else might be hidden beneath that coat?

It hid a dress, another of the clothes Hilda was saving to wear when her husband, on active Naval service, came home.

From that moment on, Hilda insisted on seeing exactly what her sister was wearing under her dress as well as under her coat before she left the house.

Did the discovery mark the end of a long-running subterfuge? No, it simply demanded a diversion. A desired dress and underwear, folded into a brown paper carrier bag, was dropped out of the bedroom window to be retrieved by Phoebe's friend and ally June Guest. The plot hatched between them went like a dream. June would come into the house carrier bag in hand, no one thinking it strange at all. Then, following the close inspection of Phoebe's apparel the accomplices would return to June's parents' home where Miss 'Pat Astbury' cheerfully donned the clothes 'borrowed' from Hilda.

The ruse went undetected for months but came at last to an end. A passion for shoes runs like a thread between Annie's daughters. We have an ongoing love affair with them, and all except Ann wear the identical size.

But during this period, only Phoebe and Hilda wore the same size and Phoebe recognised no boundary. If a thing was there to be used then she could use it regardless of whoever owned it . . . a cheeky smile and a roguish shrug of the shoulder were usually enough to get her out of any scrape, such was her charisma. Arguments with an older sister? The odd bout of fisticuffs? They slid away like water off a duck's back.

Yet it was water, or perhaps more accurately, snow, that brought matters to a head.

Hilda saved hard to buy quality and one such purchase was a pair of black suede, high-heeled shoes adorned on the front with a slim leather tassel which flipped from side to side with each step.

How Phoebe drooled, but the ultimatum was given, *Do not touch!*

The following weekend was to see a dance at

Willenhall baths. Wouldn't those shoes be just perfect?

Do not touch!

All week the ultimatum rattled in Phoebe's head as she worked making steel springs and all the while the mental picture of herself dancing in those beautiful shoes played in her mind.

The evening of the dance arrived.

Once more she thought of Hilda's words; but the lure of those dark beauties proved too strong. The shoes went out of the window along with the rest of her selection.

The evening's entertainment over, and with a new beau to see her home, Phoebe left the dance hall. During the evening it had snowed hard but then had turned to slush. This was something she had not taken into account. Her own shoes, which she had worn on leaving Dangerfield Lane, had been left along with the rest of her clothes at her friend's house! She would have to walk through the wet grey melting snow in Hilda's new shoes.

Arriving home she felt a flood of relief to find only Father waiting up, the rest of the family having gone to bed. Once she was safely indoors, Father did the same.

Phoebe looked at the sodden shoes.

How on earth could she explain this?

She looked at the fire burning low in the grate.

There was the answer to her dilemma. Place the shoes in the side oven to dry overnight and tomorrow slip them back into their box. Problem sorted.

It might have been. But the heat of the oven caused the shoes to curl into themselves, the slush dried a dull grey, and next morning they resembled nothing more than striped beetles.

Hilda was furious. Once more her precious possessions had been taken without her consent and this time her thoughtless sister was really going to answer for her conduct! Mother finally prevented a skirmish that had the makings of World War Three.

The borrowing had gone far enough. It would end right there.

Phoebe, as with each of us, might have taken little notice had this stricture come from a sister, but she would not deliberately give Mother any grief, however small or insignificant the cause. So the 'borrowing' stopped. Well, almost!

A leopard never changes its spots and Phoebe never really broke her habit of 'borrowing' for all she promised she would. Despite being warned of the error of her little white lies, she saw no real reason to refrain from doing what suited her very well.

Until one night.

Treated to a visit to the cinema by yet another admiring boyfriend, Phoebe found he was not after all to her liking. As the picture neared its end, she excused herself – a visit to the toilet might help her think of a way of avoiding having to walk home with him.

When she spotted an open window, the solution was clear: climb through and she could be away. No sooner thought than done. Agile as a cat, she found the small opening no obstacle.

Pleased with this escape, Phoebe ran along St John's Alley and into Dangerfield Lane. It was then she detected the slight noise behind her. Footsteps? Had the lad followed her from the cinema?

Ready to screech at him to go away, even to fight if necessary, she glanced behind her. No one in sight. She smiled; she must be imagining things.

But did imagination have sound? As she walked on the tapping behind her had begun again but turning revealed only emptiness. The Lane was in darkness, there was only the tease of moonlight, first offering to lift the shadows then withdrawing to add to their depth. Phoebe felt the cool hand of apprehension. Was someone hiding in those shadows?

Setting off again, she listened for the sound. Yes, there it was . . . but that was no tap of footsteps, that was the clink of metal. Her breath caught in her throat as she remembered Mother saying, 'You'll pay one day, my wench, you'll pay for tellin' lies.'

This was payment day!

Thoroughly scared she raced all the way to the

house, the sound of metal rattling behind. She threw herself inside blurting, 'The devil . . . the devil followed me, I heard . . . I heard his chains rattling.'

The devil's chains turned out to be Ann's Girl Guide belt. One more item 'borrowed' for the evening, it had come unfastened when squirming out of that toilet window and hung down her back allowing the buckle to clink against the pavement.

The lesson might not have been sweet but it was certainly short.

Phoebe blithely carried on as before: if something was there to be had why not take advantage of opportunity?

Our patience often snapped but our devotion never did. Phoebe was loved by every one of her sisters, and her death only served to strengthen that love.

22

An Addition to the Family

I have mentioned Father's partiality to an evening at the local. With his daughters past the stage of spelling 'B's' and ten-minute lessons he would spend a couple of hours playing cards or dominoes with his workmates.

Lack of money and the scarcity of beer limited the imbibing but not the pleasure of a shared game and the social interaction it provided.

One Saturday evening spent at the 'Bird-in-Hand' ended in an unusual fashion, with Father wheeling home a pram. In it was a baby of around three months old.

Where had it come from? What did he think he was doing bringing it to the house? Mother was alarmed, he could be 'had up', arrested for child stealing.

'It were outside the pub,' Father told her. 'There were nobody with it, not a soul lookin' after it; folk who can leave a babby outside a public 'ouse don't be worthy of 'avin' kids!'

But whose child was it?

Father didn't know, neither did he seem to care about the consequences of taking the child; it had been left alone, dressed in no more than a vest, and that for Father was tantamount to its having been abandoned.

The parents would surely come soon, she would explain, tell them her husband had only acted in what he thought was the child's best interest. These thoughts in mind Mother waited, expecting a knock that would herald the arrival of not only those parents but also a constable.

But no parents came. In a quandary, she eventually gave way to Father's request she bathe and feed the child. Fortunately nightgown and baby food were supplied by Hilda, whose own son was just a few months old.

What a harrowing time for Mother! Nor did it end the next day. In fact, no one knocked on our door until Monday mid morning. It seems the woman who presented herself on the doorstep smiled and said blithely, 'We knowed who it were took the babby, we knowed it were George so we d'aint worry 'cos we knowed the little 'un were in good 'ands.'

Mother's reply would not get past the editor!

Looking at this with modern eyes, we would judge it irresponsible on perhaps everyone's part – Father for taking away the child without its parents' consent, Mother for not contacting the police and especially the parents for not fetching back the baby when they knew where it was. But one word I must add for Father's sake. He was the kindest most gentle man, his only failing – if it could be called a failing – was caring for a child left alone and practically unclothed in a darkened street.

Perhaps one more glimpse of the man will help reveal that kind nature. A glass of beer, though enjoyed, was not as valued as a cigarette. Father remained a smoker all his life. The wartime shortage of tobacco caused him on occasion to mutter what he would like to do to ''Itler'.

Though none of his daughters took up smoking, each of us would be on the watch for the chance of buying cigarettes – handing him a packet of five 'Wild Woodbines' made his face light with pleasure. Every one of those slim tubes of tobacco was treasured, so much so that he even slipped the shaft of a pin through one end in order to smoke it to the last centimetre. He never asked much from life, accepting the hardships it set in his path without allowing them to breed bitterness.

This trait was most clearly illuminated when the allotments just across the road from our house became a building site. This caused quite a stir and rumours as to what was to be erected buzzed up and down the Lane like bees. First a line of sheds . . . what were they for, did something have to be stored there?

Speculation was rife, the people of the Lane standing at their garden gates of an evening discussing the question with neighbours. Speculation ran riot when a ten-foot barrier fence of wire was erected to enclose the sheds. Could the government be storing guns and ammunition there? Was it explosives? Maybe it was bombs! Everyone had their opinion, but none came near the truth. That was revealed when, one day, several canvas-covered lorries drove onto the site. The front bedroom window giving an unobstructed view of the allotments, Mother hurried upstairs to watch.

'It weren't no guns nor ammunition was unloaded from them lorries,' she told us all that evening. 'Weren't no boxes o' no sort . . . it were men.'

'Men?' Father looked puzzled. 'What sort o' men?'

'There be only one sort to my knowledge, the sort 'avin' one 'ead an' two legs!' Miffed at having her revelation doubted, Mother's reply was arch.

'How many men?'

Still a little put out by what she viewed as her husband's scepticism, Mother sniffed. 'How should I know? They 'ad them out o' them lorries an' into them buildings afore you could bat your eyes; dressed in blue-grey overalls with a yellow patch on the back, they was, an' there was soldiers in uniform an' carryin' rifles.'

Soldiers in uniform and armed with rifles! Men

shepherded quickly into those barrack-like buildings! The 'what' of those days of speculation suddenly became 'who?'

Who were those men behind that high wire fence? There could be only one answer. Prisoners of war! A trickle of nervous excitement ran in our veins. What if those prisoners broke out? That wire fence looked none too strong – we could all be murdered in our beds! This was war in close up and the inhabitants of Dangerfield Lane were none too happy.

For the first couple of weeks tension remained high, nurtured by ideas of more and more prisoners to be brought in when foundations for several pairs of buildings were laid out.

Mothers urged their children to stay well clear, themselves darting furtive glances as they passed the site on their way to shop. Those prisoners might be working quietly now, but for how long? Suspicion was everywhere, distrust and animosity so thick it could be tasted. They were the enemy, they shouldn't be seen any other way!

Such talk was understandable in the light of war, folk had lost loved ones, lives had been shattered, but hadn't the same thing happened to those men? True, they were the enemy, but they had done only what they had been told was their duty. Like our own soldiers, they had been given no choice but had been conscripted, compelled to engage in a war they probably had no wish for. Separated from family and country, their feelings could be no different from those of the hundreds of allied forces held prisoner abroad, their fears the same. Enemy they might be, but more than that, they were men and should be treated as such.

This was Father's quiet reply to any expression of anger. Piling hurt upon hurt did no good; the men who spent the evening hour gazing through that fence before being locked in for the night were seeing not what was visible but what was in their hearts.

This natural sympathy rose to a head one evening as, together at the garden gate, Father and I looked across to where the walls of four or five semi-detached houses were half built. Reaching into his pocket Father withdrew the precious packet of Woodbines. Three of the original five remained. He had allowed himself to smoke no more than two throughout the day not knowing how long it would be before he acquired another five. But the cigarette he took from the packet was not to be smoked there beside the gate.

Taking my hand he walked me the couple of yards that would see us directly opposite the enclosure, then he handed me the cigarette and said, 'Tek that across to the fence and give it to one o' them men.'

I was afraid and hesitated until he said again, 'Go on, mah babby, they won't 'urt you an' I'll be 'ere waiting of you.'

That began a practice which continued with every pack of cigarettes Father had; there was always one sent across to the fence, the lucky recipient smiling his gratitude, a gratitude shown when one evening a toy carved by a prisoner was passed to me via the guard at the gate. A ping-pong bat held a wooden chicken which, when the bat was moved, dipped its beak into a wooden glass.

Compassion created a link in the chain of peace.

23

Parties and Parades

We'd long prayed for the ending of the war and when news of victory in Europe came, it had the folk of Dangerfield Lane, like every other street in the country, dancing, singing and crying all at the same time.

With Japan observing no surrender, we were still officially at war, but for Mother and her neighbours, that fact was to prove no obstacle. They had waited long for this day and, rationing or no rationing, they were going to celebrate.

Union Jacks of every size suddenly appeared on each house, tree and lamppost. For the first time in seven years house lights gleamed like magic lanterns, curtains left un-drawn for the sheer joy of it. All of this was a fairytale for those of us kids too young to remember pre-war days, but the fairytale was not over yet. The banquet was yet to come.

Given the hardship of food rationing, those days when it was either a bag of flour or a loaf of bread but not both, when two ounces of margarine was whipped with half a cup of milk until it neared half a pound, the rare times when the butcher offered a couple of sausages or a slice of liver and, having made their choice, women hurried home with tears of gratitude, what they produced for that street party can only be thought a miracle. Everybody contributed. Chairs, stools, trestle tables, all came from Lord knows where seeing as most everything which would burn had already gone to keep houses warm the many times there was no coal to be had.

Every child had a hat that dads had made from newspapers; housework went to the wall while mothers cut sandwiches, filling them with anything that came to hand. But for kids it was the long-forgotten delights of jellies, trifles and cakes. That the jelly was made from gelatine and a bottle of Tizer or produced from a pint of water and a long-hoarded packet of 'kayli' (lemonade powder) mattered not a jot; to us kids it was sheer magic. To this day I wonder where it all came from. The flour and lard or margarine brought to Mother's kitchen where she baked, shoving trays of cakes into the oven hour after hour while neighbours carried others to be cooked in their ovens; the eggs and milk she turned into custard for trifles or small tarts, none of this will ever be forgotten.

But though our street party went with a bang, it was not enough for the folk of Dangerfield Lane. Hard as parents had worked there was one more thing planned to mark the bliss of Hitler's defeat. The fancy dress parade!

I've heard it said many times, 'What heaven takes away with one hand it gives back double with the other.'

This was true with Mother. As well as her undoubted qualities in the kitchen, she was very creative: coloured paper and a few ribbons were instantly turned into Christmas decorations and table ornaments, while a few wartime brides went to the altar with a posy or corsage Mother made from snippets of cloth. But the VE day fancy dress parade was going to prove her pièce de résistance. Her two youngest would be in that parade.

Joan, small and dainty, was a fairy queen in blue net and silver tinsel. Carrying a bit of bamboo cane wrapped in white paper with a silver star waving proudly on top, she was happy. Not so Margaret! Dumpy, self conscious in the extreme, I walked to the fairground on Catherine's Cross. Dressed in a gown made from an old sheet, a helmet, shield and staff cut from cardboard and painted with the Union Jack, yours truly represented Britannia.

24

Variation on a Theme

War might well be over but routine at St James'
School did not vary much, neither did the lesson rota.

Although a year older and having moved on a class,
I had to endure usual tasks. Monday morning and the
English assignment was to write of something that
had occurred during the weekend. This was where
imagination really had to come in, for weekends in
Dangerfield Lane held, for us youngsters anyway,
nothing different from the rest of the week. Feeling
too grown up for street games such as skipping,
hopscotch and the rest, I had excised them from
my agenda, even fire cans and pigeons had been
abandoned, replaced by hours of standing at the
garden gate chatting with girlfriends; but I hardly
wished to write of that.

However, one particular weekend did witness a
change of routine. This provided a framework for
my composition, though the written work handed in
to Mrs Walkeden in no way reflected the truth. This
is the real story.

Hilda, my eldest sister, was seventeen when she first met Bill Hutchinson. An industrial migrant from the North-East he had come to Darlaston on an engineering course.

A few days before Christmas Hilda was going with girlfriends to the Olympia Cinema, Darlaston. Not wishing to meet the boisterous groups of young men usually gathered along King Street on Saturday evenings the girls took the bypass route along Victoria Road. A little way along, some half dozen youths came bounding out of a large detached house used for student lodgings. One caught Hilda around the waist, kissing her before laughingly letting her go.

Some time later, she came face to face with a young man she suspected of being among those in Victoria Road and soundly ticked him off. He, it turned out, had been nowhere near the place. Apology turned to smiles and the two became friends; then a few months later, when Bill was drafted into the navy, they continued their association with letters.

The inevitable, of course, happened and in November 1944, when Bill was given a few days' leave, the pair married by special licence, the service being performed by the borough registrar in the presence of Mother and Father and the groom's best man, Bill Duncan.

Bill having to return to his ship twenty-four hours after the wedding left no time for a honeymoon but, war or no war, rationing or no rationing, Mother determined they would have the best wedding reception she could give. Friends and neighbours also rallied to the cause. Two cockerels found their way to Mother's kitchen, glory of glory, so did a tin of salmon and a couple of tins of peaches – no one questioned how or where from. Even Frank White, the butcher with whom Mother had registered at the outbreak of war, came up with a seven-pound-weight tin of corned beef. Sugar, margarine, flour, eggs, all were donated to help provide cakes while lemonade and gelatine were transformed into jellies, some of which, along with the tinned fruit, became trifles covered with Mother's delicious egg custard.

Restriction of time allowed no opportunity of a studio photograph recording their special day – that had to wait until the next leave.

With demobilisation and as yet no hope of a house of their own, Hilda and Bill lived with us for a while at Dangerfield Lane, only later moving to live in the North-East.

In the early spring of 1947 Bill received a letter. The younger brother whom he had seen only a couple of times in the ten years after having left Chester-le-Street was now conscripted into the Army and had written to ask could they meet before he joined his unit.

Here, except for a few white lies saying how I had

joined with my family in trying to make a stranger feel welcome in my home, the composition I handed in to Mrs Walkeden ended.

But not so the story.

Mother, having been told the contents of the letter acknowledged none of the dilemma of where was the brother to stay.

'Of course the lad must come,' she breezed, 'he can stay 'ere with us.'

Ever ready to help, she didn't stop to think how three bedrooms, one given over to Hilda and her husband, a second occupied by herself and Father, while the much smaller third was shared by Ann, Joan and myself could ever be made to accommodate another body . . . and that body eighteen years old and male!

After so many years of making do, Mother refused to recognise the existence of any bridge until she set foot on it. This one was crossed when Phoebe, who had also married, suggested two of her sisters use the sofa bed in her front room. The sisters taking up the offer were to be Ann and Joan. This left Father and Mother with their bedroom; myself, Hilda and her eighteen-month-old son, Paul, would share a second bedroom, thus leaving Bill and his brother the third one.

The day of the visitor's arrival proved a golden Friday, promising a weekend of the same warm sunny weather.

Now normally I would have welcomed an afternoon free from school, especially when it offered a trip to Birmingham; such a treat did not present itself often. However, when asked by Hilda would I go with her to the railway station I refused. This visitor had already caused enough bother by being fitted into the house and I certainly wasn't going to do anything else on his behalf.

'You will have to come!' Hilda adopted the bossy tone she had always used when demanding her younger sisters do as she told them.

But at thirteen years old and entering the stage of seeing no reason for doing anything you didn't want to, I refused again.

'You'll have to come!' Hilda repeated the order. 'I can't manage to lift Paul and the pushchair onto the bus, then carry both down all those steps leading to the station platform so you are just going to *have* to come!'

But this time the big sister act was not going to work. It was her problem, her brother-in-law, so it was up to her to sort it out! A toss of the head saying as much I made to leave for school. Hilda saw her opportunity and played her trump card.

'I can't go to bring Bill's brother from Birmingham,' she said plaintively as Mother entered the room.

'Why?' Mother asked.

'Well it's difficult enough getting on and off the buses yourself in the rush hour. With Paul and the pushchair it will be impossible, to say nothing of trying to carry both down several flights of steps to the platform.'

'Margie can go with you.'

Oldest and wisest! Hilda's glance reflected her triumph, but she wasn't finished just yet.

'I've asked her,' she said, her voice holding none of the bossy authority it had held before Mother had entered the room. 'She said she won't come.'

Her expression unruffled, Mother looked to where I stood ready to bolt through the kitchen and out of the door. She said two words, 'You're goin'!'

Two words! Two words and all conflict was ended. You did not argue with Mother.

My teenage truculence, needing an outlet it had not found during the journey to Birmingham New Street Station, was soon to realise expression.

Dark-haired, grey blue eyes smiling hello, Hilda's brother-in-law stepped from the train. Fresh from an area rich in fields and greenery he glanced about the smoke-grimed platform bathed in clouds of soot-filled steam from trains belching arrival and departure.

'So this is Birmingham?' His smile deepened.

I was resentful at being made to do something I had no desire to do, to go where I had no wish to go and I flared up. It was *his* fault! If he had not come! I glared accusingly at this stranger from a train answering tartly, 'Well if you don't like it you know what you can do!'

It was rude and deserved the anger Mother later would show when informed of my behaviour, but teenage blood had been roused. So let him go straight back home – who cared?

But the young man who introduced himself as Ralph did not go home. He stayed several days.

Mother took to him like a duck to water. He could have been the son she never had. Father, too, showed his liking for the lad who merged so comfortably with 'his wenches' . . . and as for Ralph, he had not simply met up with his brother, he had found a mother and a family of sisters.

The few days of that visit passed. I had paid little attention to the visitor, yet once he had left I found I missed him, somehow . . . inexplicably . . . I missed him.

A month or so later Mother had a letter. The lad she had taken to so strongly was to be given a week-end pass, could he come see the family?

The same upheaval ensued, as before, but this time I felt no resentment, even placidly accepting Hilda's invitation to go along with herself, her husband and his brother to the cinema.

Several weekend passes were given and each

brought Bill's brother to the house where Mother lavished affection on him and he quickly came to love her like the mother he had lost when one year old.

Then it was embarkation leave, a week before his unit was due to sail to Greece. In the intervening weeks, Hilda and Bill had moved to live with his father, who, now his younger son was called to National Service, was alone.

A week allowed time enough to return to the North-East, to be with his own father and brother; instead Ralph once again spent the week in Wednesbury.

Why was this? Why come to Dangerfield Lane when he could as easily go home? More puzzling still, why seem to want my company more than Ann's? After all, they were almost the same age. But of his new-found sisters it was me he escorted to school, me he waited for in the playground in order to walk me home, me he laughed with but didn't tease.

Saturday and Ralph must return to camp. Could I see him off at that same railway station? The train was leaving at three in the afternoon, I could be back home by four. Mother agreed.

Right on time the train gathered steam, the guard calling 'All aboard.'

The smile I had come to know touching his mouth, he took my hand and said quietly, 'This is not goodbye.'

Pinned to my lapel was a cheap pendant bought from Woolworths some time previously – a heart and a key held together by a short length of chain.

Before I was aware of what was happening, he had removed the pendant, snapping the chain so it fell into two pieces. Keeping the heart in his hand he returned the key to me.

'You are one part,' he said. 'I am the other; one day we will join the two together.'

Five years later, I married that stranger from the train and on my wedding day he gave back the heart.

Though they are black with age, I still have both pieces.

25

Monotonous Regularity

Given the long years having to count every penny, plus the added restrictions of war, it can be no wonder that many of my memories of childhood are those of happenings taking place at school. So I make no apologies for much of what I have written, and that I now continue to write consisting of the same.

Another year at school! The government had raised the leaving age to fifteen, the factory would have to wait another twelve months.

This was blow enough to a girl champing at the bit but there were other blows to come, and in the purported words of Queen Victoria's consort, 'with monotonous regularity'.

Maybe it was personality clash, but the newly appointed head teacher's disapproval had been obvious that afternoon of her first visit to the school and it had grown more than obvious ever since. Pamela Harris and I were definitely not flavour of the month. In fact, we were not flavour of the year! I still wonder what it was exactly that woman had in her craw? We could not be accused of insubordination, my upbringing had been one of 'You behaves y'self at school and ya don't answer back.' This rule laid down by Mother had been adhered to, except for the one time Joan had been about to be slapped by Miss Patrick.

Was that the reason then? Was it determination such behaviour would not occur again that lay behind actions which so many years later I see as having nothing of good intent?

One such incident took place one morning soon after assembly. Cousin Mary, in the same class as myself, was sent for. In Miss Jones' study she was shown a note.

'Will you please explain this!'

Hailstone words snapped while a glacial stare watched for any indication of guilt.

'I, I haven't seen it, Miss,' Mary answered nervously.

'I did not ask had you seen it!' Words bounced across the desk. 'I asked you to explain!'

Mary read the note again. 'It says, it says will I be going to the "Woden" tomorrow night.'

That was like waving a red rag in front of a bull. Snatching the paper across the desk, the headmistress fumed. 'I can read, child; but you, it seems, cannot understand a simple sentence so I will ask again: explain the meaning of this note.'

Thoroughly bemused Mary sat silent. What was it she was expected to say?

'How often do you visit the "Woden"?'

Relieved at being given direction, Mary replied quickly. 'Not every Thursday, Mom doesn't always let me go.'

'I see.' The frostbite stare continued. 'And when you are allowed to go, what time do you arrive there?'

'About seven o'clock.'

'And you stay how long?'

' 'Til about ten.'

Triumph gleaming on her narrow face the headmistress nodded. Her assumption was proved correct.

'I see . . . and what exactly do you do while you are there?'

Mary did not hesitate. 'We dance,' she said.

'Dance!' Heat of anger warmed the frigid tone. Was the girl being facetious?

Wanting only to be out of that room and away from the person we were all a little afraid of, Mary enlarged on her answer. 'They play music and we dance.'

Another nod. 'And where is this "Woden"?'

'Darlaston, Miss, in Franchise Street.'

Something had not quite fitted into place.

A stab of irritation evidenced by clamped lips and widely flared nostrils caused the nervous Mary to hold her breath. What was this all in aid of?

But she was asked no more questions. Dismissed with the instruction to send Margaret Astbury up to the teacher immediately Mary scuttled from the room.

Now what! Rebellion did raise its head as I tapped on a door displaying the painted lettering it had displayed in my mother's time as pupil . . . 'Headmistress. Private Room.' But I knew not to let my feelings get the better of me for there would be worse than hell to pay should reports of cheek reach Mother.

The questions I later learned had been put to my cousin were put verbatim to me until reaching that which asked the location of the 'Woden'. That came not as, 'Where is this "Woden"?' but as, 'The "Woden", that is at the High Bullen is it not?'

'No.' I shook my head. 'It isn't in Wednesbury, it's in Darlaston.'

'Where in Darlaston?'

Was this how criminals were interrogated? I was certainly beginning to feel like one.

'Franchise Street,' I answered, the mutiny inside threatening to surface. 'It's a room belonging to the Woden engineering works, they allow it to be used as a youth centre. Sometimes Mary and me go with my sister Ann.'

End of interrogation.

The note? Written by me it had been found by the

headmistress. Where had she found it? In my coat pocket.

It would have been easier to swallow had she gathered the whole class with their coats and asked each girl to separately empty the pockets. But that was not the way she played, instead she preferred to search those coats while they hung in the cloakroom. An act I find unworthy of anyone calling themselves a teacher.

Why the fuss? Why the cross examination?

'Woden' was the name of an engineering works in Darlaston but, as then unknown to Mary and myself, it was also the name given to a public house that still stands at the High Bullen in Wednesbury. It was this latter 'Woden' we were suspected of visiting on a Thursday evening. Yes, I agree a check had to be made, what I disagree with is the underhand way of discovering that note, when the same results could have been achieved without the rancid air of dishonesty and distrust.

July 1948. My last day at school. A year which for me had disproved the adage, 'School days are the best days of your life' had reached its end.

But not before the leaving party.

As a special treat, those of us who had reached their fifteenth birthday and therefore the end of compulsory education were to be allowed the privilege of changing out of the uniform which had been introduced in the last six months of an eleven-year period, and which Miss Jones insisted every pupil must have, regardless of the very limited time it would be needed and definitely regardless of a family's economic situation.

The party was to be held in the assembly hall and those of us girls who wished could provide themselves with lemonade to drink while they stood around and chatted. No music . . . no strobe lighting . . . not what you might call a disco, but the very break from everyday regime made it something to look forward to.

At four-thirty in the afternoon, prayers had been said and we were dismissed. We had half an hour to race home, change out of our navy blue skirt and green blouse, and be back at school for five o'clock.

The gown from which Hilda had fashioned a full skirt had come from the same source as other items Mother had bought from time to time, the jumble sales, but feeling the cool softness of it about my legs, seeing the pale sea pearl shot-silk taffeta gleam soft blue, pink and silver as I moved, I felt like all the princesses of the world rolled into one. Hilda's black suede peep-toe shoes (thank heaven we wore the same size) completing the transformation, I was ready. But despite my haste time had hastened more quickly, it was already five minutes to five o' clock.

The hour allowed for the party would be half over before I got there. The bus? That would already have gone and the next would not be due for half an hour. There was no coach for this Cinderella.

This was to have been a treat, a happy ending to a dismal school year and now I would miss it!

It was Mother who took the role of fairy god-mother. 'Take Ann's bike,' she smiled, 'go on, it'll be all right when her knows it were me said you could.'

I needed no second urging. Skirt tucked safely between my bottom and the saddle, I was off.

If I took the entrance which led from the boy's playground I could leave the bicycle in the space beneath the stairs leading up to the Senior department. This method of entry had always been discouraged: with Miss Jones as headmistress it was definitely banned. But who was to know? The care-taker was nowhere to be seen and sounds from above said anyone else was already in the hall; but none-theless it might be well to go quietly.

A first series of steps gave onto a small rectangular landing from which a further flight curved upward. At the top was the cloakroom. Though not a room as such, but simply a couple of wooden stands with metal coat hooks this had many times proved a sheltered haven for latecomers who could hide behind the coats.

I no longer needed to hide, to slip into school while no one was looking! This was what I told myself, but habit is not easily shrugged off and so I mounted the stairs with the tread of a cat burglar.

I had reached the landing when I heard it. There above me, at the head of the stairs – voices! In the words of the best spy fiction, my cover was blown.

Should I go back down those stairs and round to the Senior girls' playground then re-enter the school via the entrance I should have taken in the first place? Should I simply stand quietly and wait for the speakers to go away?

Hovering over the decision of which avenue to take, I heard my name spoken.

'Margaret Astbury!'

Miss Jones' finest imperious tone floated down to where I stood. Breath froze in my chest! Was I once again in trouble? For what? Being a few minutes late for a party I was not forced to attend!

'Huh!' The voice carried, slicing the air like a razor, 'Margaret Astbury . . . she will never do any good . . . she will never amount to anything.'

I could have turned back then, slipped away home with nobody any the wiser. Maybe I should have done just that, but Mother would have wanted to know the reason for my returning home just ten minutes after leaving it, she would have demanded to know the full story.

I couldn't bear that. I couldn't bear her to hear the dismissive words I had just heard, to feel the hurt I was feeling. So, the heels of Hilda's shoes tapping loudly on the stone staircase I continued to the party.

Perhaps the Oracle of Spite has been proved correct. I never tried for office in politics, medicine or any of those fields held to be of public importance. Caring for a semi-invalid mother a few years after leaving school, keeping house for parents and a sister until she married, then later combining this with looking after my own home and family, together with part-time factory work, left little time to follow any other pursuit until I reached my mid thirties. So in answer to that long-ago prediction I can only reply that while never amounting to anything, while perhaps never doing any good, I do have more letters after my name than Miss Jones had *in* her name!

26

Where There's a Will

In 1946 Phoebe, my second eldest sister, married Andrew Williams, recently demobbed after serving with a paratroop regiment in India.

Though by this time the war had ended food rationing had not, so their reception followed the same pattern as Hilda's, though that was the only similarity.

Andrew being of the Catholic faith, Phoebe changed her faith so that they could marry in St Mary's Church, Wednesbury.

It is regularly held that history has a habit of repeating itself and it certainly did here. Like her mother so many years before, Phoebe borrowed her wedding finery; Theresa, one of Andrew's cousins, lent it. The bridesmaids' dresses were also borrowed from a family living in the Lane, the daughter, Maria Woolley, being an attendant along with another friend, June Guest, myself, Ann and Joan.

Made of mauve taffeta the dresses were teamed

with white silk muffs trimmed with mauve silk rose-
buds and the headdresses were of white ruched net
and mauve ribbons.

Both families attended the wedding though
mother-in-law and bride had little love for each other;
so, following the marriage, neither visited the other
except on very rare occasions. But visits home to see
Mother were a daily occurrence, Phoebe walking the
twenty-minute journey from King's Hill to Dangerfield Lane.

Then, confined with her first child, a son Andrew,
she had to put the visits on hold.

But not only did her daughter need the support of a
mother at this time, there was also a second grandson
to cuddle. There was only one thing to be done,
Mother would go to King's Hill.

Now at this time, 1946, the Astbury family had no
car, neither did any neighbour, so the only way was to
walk. Unlike today, no bus ran along Dangerfield
Lane.

We all knew that Mother's crippled leg was trou-
bling her, that she was often in pain, but regardless of
assurance that daughter and grandson were doing
fine nothing was going to prevent her seeing them for
herself.

Saturday evening found her ready to go. Father
was apprehensive. 'It be a fair way to walk along to the
Bull Stake and on up King's Hill!' The caution was

echoed by the rest of us, but neither husband nor children were going to deter Mother.

Everything went well, mother and daughter weeping happily in each other's arms, grandfather and father just as happily indulging themselves by following tradition and 'wetting the baby's head' across at the nearby Old Barrel pub.

It was when Mother and Father set off to come home that things began to veer slightly off course.

'Going back the way we come be all around the Wrekin!' Father indicated the unnecessary length of their journey. 'We can cut across the cornfields and be 'ome in five minutes.'

A logical suggestion, unless you take into account the cornfields he referred to had seen no corn for many years and had long since served as a tipping ground for molten slag thrown out by iron foundries and steel works . . . and add to this the consideration of it being eleven o' clock at night, with the proposed route having no such thing as street lighting.

But this was a small price to pay set against the advantage of a much reduced journey. At least so Father said.

Saying and doing, as we all have learned at one time or another in life, can be poles apart, and for Mother that Saturday evening seemed to prove just that. The ground was rough and uneven, the path a narrow track pitted with sharp lumps of solidified molten waste. Father, sure on his feet as a mountain goat and with sight that could see the clock tower of St Bartholomew's Church over a mile from the house, found no difficulty manoeuvring his way. Holding Mother's hand, encouraging her every step, he led the way.

Halfway down a sharp rise the steps halted.

In some pain Mother could go no further. Perhaps a short rest, a moment or two to get her breath. A moment or two spread to a minute or two, then on to five. It was no use, Mother could not put weight on her crippled leg.

What to do? It was as far to walk back to Phoebe's house as it was to reach the end of the field and the ground was equally rough.

In the near distance, illuminated by a shaft of moonlight spilling between low hanging clouds, Father could see the dark outline of the Donkey Bridge which carried a railway goods line. Just beyond was Woden Road West; the metalled surface would be easier for Mother to walk on.

'It might as well be the moon, for I can't walk to that neither!' Mother's reply to the urging they were halfway to the road was sharp and decisive. She could walk no further!

She could not walk nor would she agree to being carried; one slip on this ground and they could both finish up with broken limbs.

There was sense in that. Father weighed the situation in his mind. If they both got hurt they would be stuck here until workmen using the path to get to the outlying factories found them on Monday morning, the family presuming they were staying the weekend with Phoebe.

But where was the sense in standing here in the middle of a field if he didn't really have to?

Pulling off his jacket, setting it and Mother on the ground, he disappeared into the darkness.

He had left her alone! Alone in the middle of a field! Alone in the dark! Mother's lip trembled. There could be all sorts of creepy crawlies around. There could be feral cats, they were known to roam this field. Her lips wobbled harder. How could he do such a thing as leave her here on her own, why had he done it?

A little way off a sound broke the stillness of the night.

Mother's lip caught between her teeth.

A cat . . . a dog . . . a man?

Each probability sharpened the fear that already had her heart hammering. If only she could hold the fear in, manage not to cry out, then perhaps whatever was there in the darkness would go away.

But it did not go away.

A second sound, a third! Mother pressed her knuckles to her mouth. Something . . . someone . . . was coming toward her.

Then as another waterfall of moonlight cascaded over the edge of a black cloud, lighting the field around her, she saw – a horse. The sounds which had so terrified her were being made by a horse, and leading it was Father.

'I think the Blessed Virgin Mary must 'ave felt much like meself when her were carried on a donkey to Bethlehem . . . 'cept I were not pregnant.' Mother would smile, recalling the episode in the days which followed. 'Your dad remembered Weaver's 'orse were put to graze on ground bordering where the railway line passes the top of the Lane. It took no more than a few minutes following the rails to get there and back but to me sittin' on me own in the dark it seemed more like a few lifetimes. I just be thankful we met nobody as we came the rest of the way, me sittin' on the back of that 'orse.'

Where there is a will there is a way; but Father knew had he told Mother of his idea to borrow Weaver's horse then her will might have proved his plan to have no way!

27

Countdown

Mother, you might have decided for yourself, was
friendly to a fault but blind she most definitely was
not. She did see through one person, or at least
through the wool he attempted to pull over her eyes.

Caught by the government raising the school-leav-
ing age to fifteen, I was in the last few weeks of this
not-so-enjoyable final year.

One late July afternoon I was sent to collect a
supply of needlework threads from the haberdashery
shop in Upper High Street which ran through the
centre of Wednesbury town. It was a small, poky,
dimly lit establishment which for me had a slightly
nerve-tingling feel to it.

But the man who stood behind the counter smiled
as I entered. Dressed in dark suit and a white shirt
with stiff collar, he nodded on hearing what it was I
had come to buy. Consulting the list I handed him, he
produced a shallow drawer filled with carefully
placed threads, his manner pleasant and talkative.

'What was my name . . . which class was I in?'

More tray-like drawers of thread were produced, placed on the counter one after another, colour being held against colour, shade compared to shade.

'Did I like school? When would I be leaving there?'

Glancing at the paper upon which the headmistress had written the number and colours of the required embroidery threads trays were exchanged for yet more trays and the process of selection began again and with that more questions.

'What did I like to do after school? Did I have many friends? Perhaps one special friend?'

No other customer had come into the shop, no one was waiting to be served . . . perhaps that was the reason the man was spending so much time sorting my order.

A tray of green threads was replaced by another, its contents a rainbow of reds ranging from deep plum to palest flesh pink.

'Where did I live?'

It is easy now to say I ought not to have been so forthcoming with my answers, but that had not been the way my parents taught. 'Answer honest an' civil when spoken to' was their creed and I followed it that afternoon.

'Had I thought of the kind of employment I might take?'

I had not. I just had this rosy dream of being free of the restrictions of school and its haughty, ever critical new headmistress, who on her introductory visit announced she had 'taught at the school where Princess Margaret was a pupil'. That I think paints the picture of Miss Jones.

'Have your parents anything in mind? Have they decided upon a job for you?'

Had they? Hilda and Phoebe had gone straight into a factory, Ann eventually doing the same. That had been a sore point with Mother. Having had one daughter who had passed the Eleven Plus examination and for whom she had struggled to buy uniform and books only to see that same daughter give up any chance it could have afforded of a job other than in a factory, she flatly refused to do the same when I, in my turn, passed the examination.

I suppose I must have looked a little blank, this time having no ready answer.

'Would you like to work in a shop? Would you like to work here in this shop? I would make you manageress, you would be in charge.'

A short distance away the clock of the Parish Church chimed the hour. The ire of Miss Jones would be visited upon me for taking so long about a simple errand. As I explained to the shopkeeper I must hurry, he smiled. He would telephone the school to say the bill for the threads would be in the post, that it was entirely due to him that I had taken so long.

'I would be manageress, Mom, the man said if I go to work in that shop he would make me manageress!'

It sounded so important and I was so full of it I didn't notice Mother was less keen.

The rest of the week passed as usual, no more being said of the proposed position at the haberdashery shop. Then Saturday lunchtime the man arrived on our doorstep.

Invited in, he was as pleasant with Mother as he had been with me and when Father arrived home from work he enthusiastically joined in the discussion as to which horse stood the better chance of winning the Grand National that afternoon. I have vague memories of their settling upon one they thought most suited to win, though there is nothing vague about the memory of my displeasure when I was handed a betting slip and several coins. Placing a bet was a daily event with Father and we all hated having to take the money around the corner to Rachel Turner, the bookie who lived in Banfield Road; at present that chore was mine and I disliked it more than a little. Handed the bet, as always placed in an envelope, Father repeated the daily instruction: 'If you see a policeman put it in the post box.' This stood quite handy right outside of the Turner house and I guess it often saw service as a disposal chute, for street betting of any kind was illegal.

Mother thanked her visitor for the shilling he

offered me as reward for taking the bet he too had made but said firmly it was not required.

The man stayed the whole afternoon, listening with Father to the race broadcast over the wireless Mother had purchased on the 'strap' soon after the start of the war. Paying sixpence a week at that time may have been extravagant but it had been a link to what was happening, a way of hearing the latest news, nine o' clock in the evening becoming almost a sacred time we children had never dared interrupt.

Around five o' clock, drinking tea and eating a slice of Mother's home-made cake, he broached once more the reason for his visit, outlining the opportunity it afforded. 'Where else might a girl of fifteen hope to be offered such a position? As manageress she would be in sole charge of the shop, surely you can see the advantage of this, and the salary, that would reflect her position.'

One after the other he presented the pros of my accepting employment in that shop, both parents offering no comment, asking no question until, smiling, their visitor said he was sure I would like what was being offered.

'Mebbe her would,' Mother answered as the man's smile switched to me. 'And I thanks you for the trouble you took in comin' 'ere but her'll be tekin' no job in that shop.'

'But she would be in charge, manageress.'

'In charge of who?' Mother's interruption was

crisp. 'Manageress over how many? There be only one works in that shop and that one be y'self! The answer still be no, her will be tekin' no job there.'

I was given no explanation of the refusal, no reason for why I was not to be allowed to accept the position of manageress in a haberdasher's. Mother's lips were firmly clamped as she showed her visitor to the door. For myself, as for my sisters, it was leave school on Friday afternoon and begin work in an engineering factory. I never did ask the reason of her refusing to allow me to take employment at the draper's shop; but now older, and hopefully wiser, I am glad she answered as she did.

These snippets of childhood memories speak of two people whose struggle to rear five children was very real. My story tells not of financial wealth, the security money can give, but I hope it reveals the character of my parents. Their hands were always ready to help, their commonsense attitude there to guide, their confidence in their children forever strong.

That confidence, always there to whisper support in my ear, has been the mainstay of my life; it was and is the prop which holds me up whenever I falter.

This last is not a childhood memory but it is one that I think illustrates the regard other people had for my parents.

Forty years after leaving school, my husband and I paid a nostalgic visit to St James' School, myself gazing at the classrooms I remembered so well while he stood again in the playground where, as a newly drafted soldier, he had waited for that very young girl to finish lessons for the day. Forty years had passed, yet suddenly it was only yesterday.

One visit led to another, so next it was to Dangerfield Lane and a slow drive past the house which held so many memories. Beginning the return home, following the Portway Road, we stopped at the Nelson pub, an establishment which, though I had passed it in childhood, I had never entered.

After a little while a man came in to buy his drink and stood with it at the bar, looking to where we sat. He stared so much that I began to feel very out of place. Could it be that we were not welcome? It was a very old pub and maybe its regular customers viewed strangers as intruders.

Determined to leave, I was reaching for my bag when, still standing at the bar, the man called, 'Be you one of the Astburys?'

Surprised, I nodded.

'Did you know the Astburys who lived in Danger-field Lane?'

Again I nodded.

'The mother had a crippled leg?'

Who was this man? He was no one I recognised, yet he seemed to know my parents.

Another nod and he crossed to us, asking again, 'You knew them?'

'Yes.' I spoke for the first time. 'George Astbury was my father, his wife Annie was my mother.'

At this the stranger wriggled himself on to the seat between my husband and me and continued to ply me with questions. At last, satisfied I was who I claimed to be, he said he had worked alongside Father at Newman's Tubes. Then standing up, he took my hand and, shaking it, said quietly, 'If you be half as much a lady as your father were a gentleman then I be proud to meet you.'

One man's tribute to another. I will never forget those words.

There is no headstone marking the graves of Annie and George, no carved image to their memory. Theirs is a tribute that cannot be seen for it is carried in the hearts of their children; it is a living, breathing memorial of love, the love they gave to me and my sisters, and in turn to their grandchildren. No recompense was asked, no rule laid down other than we do right by each other and do nobody a bad turn.

It was no easy life for them, struggling to support a

growing family, but it was one they filled with love and happiness for five daughters. We each know what we owe to them, we each remember, and every day we whisper, 'I love you, Mom, I love you, Dad.'

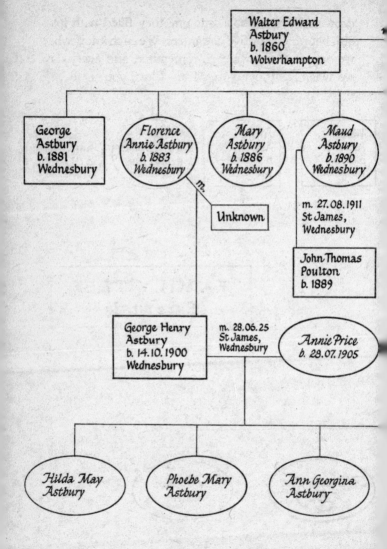

Mary Eliza ?
b. 1863
Birmingham

Walter
Astbury
b. 1893
Wednesbury

Alfred Ernest
Astbury
b. 19.10.1893
Wednesbury

Edith
Gertrude Astbury
b. 07.03.1897
Wednesbury

Beatrice
May Astbury
b. 03.11.1904
Wednesbury

FAMILY TREE
(Paternal)

Margaret Rose
Astbury

Irene Joan
Astbury

Bibliography

Tipton, Wednesbury and Darlaston in Old Photographs compiled by Robin Pearson. (Gloucester: A. Sutton 1989)

Wednesbury in Old Photographs compiled by Ian M. Bott (Stroud: Sutton 1994)

Wednesbury Revisited by Ian M. Bott (Stroud: Sutton 1998)

Hops and Hop-Pickers by Christine Faulkner (Brierly Hill: Faulkner 1992)

Photographic credits